AF322712

KIMBERLEY MENDOZA

The Awakening

Conquering Wickedness Through the Mighty Name of Jesus

This is dedicated to the future generations of leaders that will have a heart set on fire for Christ.

Contents

Preface

The people of this world have succumbed to their troubles and have masked themselves in darkness. They have a void in their heart they fill with loneliness. Their life is full of ungodly traits. God warns us we shall know them by their fruits. Who is your master, and who do you really serve? People are blinded and influenced so much by evil.

As the church of Christ, take up your sword to defeat and conquer wickedness at its core. It is time to wake up to the truth. You will read a revelation about Satan's tactics of deception toward us while learning how to use the authority that you have to conquer it. I show you how to be guided in your walk with God and how to rebuke whilst standing your ground upon the rock that is Christ. I will unveil the truths about the darkness that surrounds us in this world and how to fight against it. Read with an open mind as I dig deep into the New Age, witchcraft, divination, and so much more. We, as warriors of Christ, need to rise and use our authority.

Acknowledgement

I want to express my deepest gratitude to my sister for her tremendous work in my ministry. Expressing countless hours and days on this project to bring it to life for the purpose of spreading my message to the nations. This endeavor would not have been possible without your continuous sacrifice that has been made for this book.

1

I am Who I am

We always speak and reference God as the God who made the heavens and the earth. He is the God who created man and all the animals on the earth, and that's often the extent of what everyone knows of God. My question to you is, do you really know who He is?

It seems so long ago now, when I was about thirteen years old, I discovered who God is. I remember I was in my room on a normal day and my sister came to ask me if I died where would I go, to Heaven or Hell? It stunned me when she asked me because I wasn't prepared for such a question. After all, I was only thirteen years old. She went into more detail with her question, which I cannot remember. All my past trauma affected my memory, and I have written about these events in my last book. I remember her telling me about God and about Jesus being in my life. That Jesus was the only way to bring me to Heaven if I accepted him into my heart with conviction. I pondered upon what she was saying as it got me thinking. Accepting Jesus into my life would make me new and would save me. Was it really that easy to be saved from Hell? Was my life really going to change after that day? She asked me a question, "Would you like to accept Jesus as your Savior?" I said yes. I repeated after her in the prayer we did and, just like that, with conviction I was saved. Realistically, as someone so young, I never knew how my life would go. I knew I had this person named Jesus who I had just accepted into my life. Little did I know angels rejoiced in that instant as it says in the bible. I can't even imagine what that looks like, rejoicing as an angelic being over a sinner coming to Christ. In the same chapter of Luke chapter 15 verse seven, it says that there is joy in heaven over one sinner repenting.

Luke 15:7 (KJV)
I say unto you, that likewise, joy shall be in heaven over one sinner that repenteth, more than over ninety and nine just persons, which need no repentance.

Luke 15:10 (KJV)
Likewise, I say unto you, there is joy in the presence of the angels of God over one sinner that repenteth.

In order to reach the kingdom of God, it takes more than goodness; it requires salvation. We cannot expect ourselves to be with God in heaven by doing good deeds alone. Good deeds are nothing if you are living a life without Christ in your heart.

You must have the conviction of understanding that without God, we are nothing. The one who gives us this conviction is the Holy Spirit. People must understand what conviction means. It's realizing that we need Christ. He died on the cross for our sins, and we need him to abide in our lives. Once we have Christ in our lives, we receive the Holy Spirit who leads us in all truth and convicts us of our sins or when we are in the wrong. It's the work of the Holy Spirit in us that produces this new life. The Holy Spirit guides us every day in all we do. That little voice that tells you what's right and what's wrong isn't a voice in your head, but the Holy Spirit.

With Christ, we have forgiveness and his everlasting love and mercy. Even without Christ, we are living in a time of mercy and God loves us without fault, but that doesn't get us saved from an eternal life of torment. What saves us is having Jesus in our lives, believing that Christ died on the cross and arose on the third day. We must receive the Holy Spirit that was promised and have our names written in the book of life. Our repentance is what saves us and the way to keep our salvation is by maintaining our relationship with God.

We are all given the opportunity to repent and to accept Christ into our lives. Do not wait until it is too late. Death comes into our lives without notice. I urge you to live a life with Christ in your heart because you cannot guarantee tomorrow.

As time went on, I discovered what the love of God truly was. Nothing compares to that first love that you have in the Lord.

I began learning piano and what it was to walk with the Lord in every way. After coming home from bible class or a normal church service, I would insist that my sister teach me the works of the Lord. There were a million questions I had for her and that resulted in her giving me her own lessons on God and who he was. I had this yearning to discover the most I can about my Lord, and it was wonderful. I would not trade those early days of seeking the Lord for anything. We should all yearn for his presence as we all do when we first come to Christ in the early days of our walk with him.

My early encounters with spiritual warfare took place in my dreams in the spirit realm. And as stated in my previous book, God gave me discernment. Because of my discernment and how much I was seeking God at this stage of my life, I would see and feel demonic forces when others could not. I never got it as impactful as my sister did, even with the encounters described in my last book.

Here, throughout this book, I will unveil different attacks that the enemy had conjured up against my life. I'll describe these spiritual attacks I've experienced in the spirit world as mentioned before.

As you read this book, I ask the Lord if there is someone who is a nonbeliever of Christ, that God can illuminate your mind and reveal himself to you. I pray in Jesus' name that this book speaks to at least one person and that this book can minister to the lives of this generation. May we all come together for our fellow brothers and sisters in Christ in unity. Praying against the evil that roams this world, that the Lord can continue to show his Glory to all. Lord, break the chains of deception, the chains of the oppressed, and free those bounded by the grasp of Satan in Jesus' name. Amen.

2

JEHOVA RAPHA

In my last book, I went into great detail about my battery case in the Resistance chapter. It was a horrible sequence of circumstances, one after the other. Throughout that process, I knew deep down that my case would go nowhere. It did, however, leave deep wounds that I never took a grasp of.

The act of the battery towards me took place in January right before my birthday. There were so many things that happened to me that year, but that night is one I never recovered from. It wasn't because of the act itself, but because of when it happened.

This crime happened around my birthday and because of that, my birthday represented everything filthy. The day I was born now represented this foul act. It marked me. What should be a great day to celebrate instead made me feel repulsive in every way.

Every year after my attack, I made it my mission to make my birthday greater than the last. I was trying to find some way to make myself feel exhilarated. Before my birthday would come up, I always stopped eating for a few days. I would lose my appetite without even realizing why. At first, I didn't realize it. When I did, it sickened me to think that I would even feel this way. Throughout the entire year, I'm always thinking of ways to celebrate my upcoming birthday. Let me break this down further. I would spend all summer and all year configuring ways to be happy on my birthday. Normal people wouldn't spend more than a few minutes at most thinking of plans for themselves, let alone months. I became obsessed with redeeming what was supposed to be a normal happy day for most people.

Year after year it became the same thing. The same repetition of excessive planning. When my birthday finally came, I still felt an empty void filled with disgust, filled with deepened despair. No amount of balloons could take away the disgust within me, no amount of cake healed this pain I felt. My soul felt so disturbed and sickened. It felt like a slow creeping poison traveling through these veins of mine, crippling me. It was a slow, agonizing sensation of pain throughout the years. The injustice in my case left me with this sadness that never mends.

There came a time after a few years when I just accepted reality. My birthday would never satisfy me. I came to believe that I would always be this person who reeked of pain every year. People may not even have noticed what I was feeling because I don't display my pain to anyone, and I never did.

I don't expect normal, sound-minded people with no physical harm done to them to understand what I mean, which is why I speak about it now. I speak to you about how I felt so that if you shall ever encounter someone of the same temperament as mine, you may talk to them with compassion and understanding. Offer words of life to people who were hurt physically, not words of hate and destruction. For we have the power to destroy someone or to uplift someone.

Proverbs 18:21 (NIV)
The tongue has the power of life and death, and those who love
it will eat its fruit.

Six years after this ongoing mess with my birthday, it was 2022, and they invited our youth group to another church's youth camp. I thought little of it even as the date drew closer. The entire year had been terrible for me. A few of our youth group went to spend the weekend at this camp near Tampa. Well, it was more like the middle of nowhere, to be exact.

I do not have pleasant experiences in camps since I always get sick. Throughout this camp, I had my usual pains throughout my body since I still had everything wrong with my body, as stated in my last book. It wasn't as bad as it could have been, so I was happy about that. Throughout the weekend, we all worshiped the Lord and sought him out as we were in a camp to do just that and to receive blessings.

Friday night's service came to a close and the music and everything was marvelous and great. Lots of youth already were getting blessed and receiving blessings left and right, and the night ended.

Saturday arrived, and there was a lot of food at this camp. For whatever reason, I felt very bloated throughout the day as I was not used to eating the foods that were given to me.

Since I had my gallbladder removed, my body doesn't take lightly to my diet being changed. As the evening service approached, I started feeling worse and worse. I didn't feel horrible till after the night service ended; I was at least able to enjoy the service. When I am bloated for a prolonged period, I feel nauseous afterward.

Throughout the Saturday night service, God's presence was moving all around us. There was an invited guest singer who came. When it was his time, he took the mic and began singing a song of his, and he began speaking to the youth.

He made an altar call for someone specific and said, "There is someone here who has been raped, molested, or hurt. If this is you come to the altar because God wants to heal you today."

He went on to say, "Where are you? Where are you? God is calling for you."

When he spoke before he could even speak two words out of his sentence, I felt this power descend upon me and I knew that the person he was calling for was me. When I felt God's presence and power come upon me, I didn't care who was watching, as there was a lot of youth in this camp. I didn't care what they would say about me. I got out of my seat and began walking to the altar towards this minister.

I never asked to be relieved of this, nor did I pray about this specifically. For the past few months, I had been fasting every week for a change to happen. It never crossed my mind that this would be my answer from God. I stood there crying, asking myself, how do I live without thinking about my attack anymore? What does that even feel like to live each day without that hindering me anymore?

I always thought that what I felt was what everyone felt after a spiritual attack. I always figured that it was part of the process to feel like utter trash within myself, but the devil is a liar. God opened my eyes, and I realized the truth. The root of my problems and feelings was that God had not healed that part of my life yet. That incident had not been taken care of the way it should have been. There was still brokenness within me. He brought to light and made known what I needed; supernatural healing.

I began to cry and cry under the presence of God and someone put their hand over my heart and began praying for me. At that moment, what had marked me for the last six years was gone, in Jesus' name. I never knew I could get rid of this sickening feeling that was in my heart. I never even knew how bad it was until He healed me and made me new. He healed a wound that had remained hidden and was slowly paralyzing me like a virus. God has the last word over our lives.

During this liberation, it felt like someone went inside of me and dissected a cancer out of me. A cancer that I never knew was there. When God set me free from it, I felt peace. I felt liberated and finally knew what it was not to be held back by this anymore. I was set free through the power of Christ and liberated from all the evil intentions and lies of the enemy. For there is power in the name of Jesus, no other name but Jesus.

Exodus 15:26 (NIV)
> *For I am the Lord who heals you.*

Psalms 34:18 (NIV)
> *The Lord is close to the brokenhearted and saves those who are*

crushed in spirit.

After this church service was over, I felt the illness getting pumped up by 100%. To make matters worse, the leaders of the camp wanted to continue with a bonfire as part of their planned events. After putting my sweater on, I walked with my youth group toward the bonfire. By this time, I felt so sick, I didn't think I could stand it anymore. I tried to pull through for a few more minutes but ended up vomiting and going back to my cabin, accepting defeat by this sickness I felt. As I mentioned earlier, I always end up sick during camp. I guess it's my fate. Sunday seemed to come so fast. Then, just like that, the camp was over, and I headed home.

Unfortunately, everyone who went to camp in our group got sick with the flu or something close to it. I felt like I was dying in bed along with my brother. At the end of the day, it was worth it to receive my blessing of freedom.

Afterward, I began researching what the biblical significance was of the number six. I was curious since seven signifies completion or perfection. What does six mean? Six represents weakness or imperfection. What's great about all of this is what the Bible says about our weaknesses.

2nd Corinthians 12:10 (NIV)
  That is why, for Christ's sake, I delight in weaknesses, in insults, in hardships, in persecutions, in difficulties. For when I am weak, then I am strong.

For six years, I was in a weakened state. But we serve an almighty God, and He is never late. Even in my weakness, God glorified his power in my life and made me strong. For in Christ, we are strong. In Christ, we are made new and whole again.

All of this was only possible because I had faith that the Lord was going to do something in my life. In the Bible, it states that Faith is the substance of things hoped for, the evidence of things not seen. When I feel myself losing hope, I begin to fast and pray to God that he would give me hope because, without having hope, how can we have faith? When I recognize that this is happening, I always ask God to give me hope because the last thing I want to do is lose my faith. Ever since I changed the way I pray, it has given me clarity on why people's prayers aren't being answered. It's simple. Some people are not praying for the right things. It can also be that people nowadays are not even praying correctly. It says in the Bible that we should ask God for wisdom. Wouldn't you want to continue to walk with Christ, but without foolishness? How many circumstances could we, as Christians, have avoided if we only asked God for wisdom? Below I'll put in some Bible references for everything that I have spoken about.

James 1:5(NKJV)
  If any of you lacks wisdom, let him ask of God, who gives to all liberally and without reproach, and it will be given to him.

Hebrews 11:1 (NKJV)
  Now faith is the substance of things hoped for, the evidence of things not seen.

Isaiah 41:10 (NIV)

So do not fear, for I am with you; do not be dismayed, for I am your God. I will strengthen you and help you; I will uphold you with my righteous right hand.

Isaiah 40:31 (NKJV)

But those who wait on the Lord shall renew their strength; They shall mount up with wings like eagles, they shall run and not be weary, they shall walk and not faint.

As I write this, it is now November. My birthday is in January and I can say with all sincerity, that I don't even think about what grand plans I have to make me feel better. I don't dwell on unnecessary thoughts that were from the devil himself. I don't even fathom the thought of my birthday anymore and the only one who did that was God. If anything, I'm looking forward to my first birthday being freed. God is who liberated me and healed my brokenness, which is why I titled this chapter Jehovah Rapha. Rapha is Hebrew for the Lord who heals. The Lord who mends. It's amazing the things we can uncover by just studying scripture, and I cannot think of any other name for this chapter but Jehovah Rapha. He healed what was dark and turned everything into light, purified me, and rid me of the lies and manipulation of the enemy. It is important that people know what it means to truly understand the God that we serve.

3

Spiritual Warfare

Into the Spirit

The more involved a person is with God, the more attacks from the enemy they will receive. Throughout our journey with Christ, there will often be times when we feel overwhelmed. However, God never gives us more than we can handle. God's word never fails. We must try to walk in God's perfect will. In this life, we have our own free will and there is also the perfect will of God. We are free to choose our own path. If we deviate ourselves from God's perfect will, we end up getting ourselves into situations that God did not plan for us to be in.

In part two of this book, I will give with great detail my personal experiences of spiritual warfare alongside tactics on how to defeat and conquer evil with the authority given to us by God.

When we begin our walk with God, we want to learn everything there is about the Lord and have personal experiences with him. We often

13

aren't told enough about how to deal with evil, and evil arrives to attack us.

I see a lot of Christians who have had the experience of waking up in the spirit world, not knowing how to deal with the spirit realm. This can happen to newborn Christians as well. It's not only Christians who find themselves in contact with the spirit realm. There are several spiritual movements and beliefs that attempt to teach and promote contact with the spirit world. The Occult and the New Age movement are just a couple. There are many others that have teachings that are not of God and some are Satanic in origin.

I will describe my own experiences and will often refer to this spirit world or spirit realm, describing it as a literal place. In this realm, there are spiritual entities such as demons, angelic beings, and also other spiritual things. Only the Spirit of God can reveal these to you and allow you to see them. When we are fighting or dealing with spiritual entities, this is the world where our battles take place. The book of Ephesians tells us we do not war against flesh and blood, but that our battles are against the rulers of darkness, against powers, and against principalities. Those who are deep into the works of God know this, but for those who aren't, I will dig deeper for a moment into the specifics of the spirit world. This is where God can reveal to us many things when he takes us there through his spirit. We must learn to see not with our physical eyes, but with our spiritual ones.

God can allow us to go through different encounters and reveal to us demonic beings. There have been some instances where I have fallen asleep unexpectedly and ended up being in the spirit world. There is an encounter where God revealed to me, I was being watched. I shall tell you about that experience.

I woke up and quickly knew I was in a place where it was barren, almost like somewhere near a desert type of environment. The wind was shuffling ever so slightly as I looked around. I saw a ragged-looking bush and behind the bush, I saw this gremlin or imp type of creature. This creature looked exactly the same as what's in the Harry Potter movies. In the movie, he guides Harry along his journey for a reference to the creature that I speak of. I saw this creature and noticed the look of hatred it had towards me, but all it was doing was watching me from afar. Once God revealed this to me, I woke up suddenly. This encounter is an example of what I refer to when I say God can choose to reveal to us demonic forces through the spirit world. Just to clarify, when we have these experiences where we find ourselves in the spirit world, I'm referring to our spirit being there, not our own body, but through spirit.

This is also where our spiritual warfare takes place when we go into battle. When we are in heavy spiritual warfare, we do not see everything that takes place in the atmosphere. We can have encounters in the spirit world or in our daily life. Jesus gave us tools to use in these situations, and we must be prepared to use them. We have these tools since the moment we accept him as our Lord and Savior.

This next encounter happened years ago. I found myself in the spirit world using the name of Jesus to conquer evil.

I remember a very long time ago, one night as I fell asleep, I found myself in the spirit world. It was a strange experience for me. When I awakened in the spiritual world, I found myself in a house that I'd never been to before. I looked around to find any familiarity and found none. There was a woman with curly hair chanting something almost like a mumble. I realized she was doing an incantation. As she was chanting to demons, she looked up at me and, without warning, demons flocked to the room. The strange thing is that they were in the form of fish, yes you read that right, fish. They were swimming in front of my feet, coming in and out through the walls, and all that they did was swim back and forth.

The woman's incantation became louder, fiercer, and she stared at me with such evil! Suddenly everything stopped, and I was standing there, and I was in the center of the room when a force yanked my spirit out of my body! My spirit was ripped out from the center of my body and at that very instant, I felt almost disabled. I can't explain to you the pain I felt having my spirit ripped out of my body. Imagine having your heart torn out of your body! Gasping for air at that very moment, trying to keep my sanity, I felt such a hurt that is unexplainable. At that very moment, I felt a dark and evil presence descend into the room and the air was so heavy, so thick, that I couldn't breathe.

It's hard to describe, but I couldn't move. I couldn't control or move my body much. I felt almost paralyzed. As all of this happens, I look to the right of me towards the floor, and I'm horrified by what I saw. I saw my body on the floor, dying, not being able to breathe, and my eyes had a purple ring around them. Surrounding the eyes was just purple from lack of oxygen and watching my body get hurt and die was horrifying to watch. I can remember my body looking up at me, trying to reach its hands outward toward me. My mind was a complete blank because the devil had blanked my mind, but I heard a voice that said two words, "rebuke", and "Jesus". I rebuked in the name of Jesus. It was so hard to even do anything because I was hurting so badly, and my body was slowly losing life! I kept rebuking them and then all at once, the fish disappeared and the demons flying around the room were leaving! There was one furious demon left and as it was leaving, it gave me a BIG push, threw me to the floor and I fell pretty hard to the ground, but

I knew the enemy had left, and my spirit was at last in peace. When it threw me, it exerted a supernatural force of momentum, pushing me to the ground. I woke up the next morning, and I noticed on the right side of my hip there was a very blackened bruise from my spiritual attack. It was the first time that I've received a visible injury from an attack, but I was glad that was over with.

This encounter that I had received was quite eventful, but even in the midst of it all, I still remembered the name of Jesus, and we must never forget how to fight the enemy even when we have our minds blanked out during our fights. This is an example of what to do if you ever find yourself sleeping one day and awakening to a battle in the spirit world. I write of these couple of encounters so that if you relate to any of this, then you may learn and start rebuking in the name of Jesus. Once you discover the true power and authority that is in Jesus' name, it will be life-changing.

When we have spiritual encounters, whether it happens when we fall asleep or when we are awake, we must use the authority given to us by God to defeat the evil in this world.

When we have encounters in real-time, not in the spirit, we must use the authority given to us to defeat the enemy.

You could be at home minding your own business when suddenly you feel a change in the atmosphere, or a presence other than God has entered your home as an example. Remember that there is power in Jesus' name. Rebuke the evil that has entered your home in the name of Jesus and the demons have to flee! Lots of people, even Christians, don't truly understand how much power and authority there is behind one name, Jesus. It says in the bible that his name is above every name.

Since the name of Jesus is above every other name, whom shall we fear? Many times, when the enemy attacks us repeatedly, the devil tries to instill fear in us, thus taking away our peace from the Lord. I know there are many Christians who the devil torments and attacks frequently, who can't find peace in their situation. If you call out the name of Jesus, you will find peace.

Philippians 2:9-10 (KJV)

Wherefore God also hath highly exalted him, and given him a name which is above every name, that at the name of Jesus, every knee should bow, of things in heaven, and things in earth, and things under the earth.

We can also see angels in the spiritual or with our spiritual eyes. If God reveals them to us and allows us to see angels, then we will see angels. We may never ask to see them, yet God may choose to reveal them to you. It all depends on the relationship that you have with God and what His will is for your life. One time, I was feeling like I was going to fall while acting out a church play of sorts one Sunday evening many years ago. The play or skit was me being an angel fighting off a demon. In this skit, I was being pushed back and forth by the supposed demon, but this person was much taller than I was, and that allowed this person to exert much more force than needed towards me without realizing it. In a split second, I was falling backward. Around this time, I was only about fourteen years old, and before I would have fallen, I felt two hands placed on my back. I knew there was nobody around me or behind me during this time. I looked behind me and there was nobody there, just to confirm my curiosity. These hands pushed me back up, preventing me from falling, and I knew after looking back that it was an angel sustaining me. I never once asked for these things to be revealed to me, but it just happened in an instant. God can use angels as a messenger or to fight in our favor.

These are just a couple of spiritual warfare experiences that I've had a very long time ago. A lot of Christians are trying to dive deeper into what they consider the unknown. People want to find new experiences with God or be in the spirit to discover more. We are not called to enter the spirit world at will. In the next chapters, I go deep into different demonic rituals and engagements. People try to take part in these activities to get into the spirit world. Trying to have unlimited access to this unknown world is demonic, and the Bible does not teach us to be there whenever we feel like it. We are called to be followers of Christ and live as he did when he was down on earth. Be very cautious in the acts and habits that you pick up over the internet. They plaster these rituals all over TV and can lead many Christians astray or ultimately cause them to stop growing in the Lord. As you prepare to read the following chapters, read them with an open mind, especially if you follow the practices that I will mention.

4

New Age

The unknown is very alluring to many people, and they will go to great lengths to satisfy this itch of curiosity. One of these curiosities is a desire to go deeper into the spiritual world. Many people want to have a deep connection with a higher consciousness. They take part in many types of rituals, seeking to unlock this energy in their lives.

We, as Christians, can be in the spirit world, but we should not try to do so by our own choosing. We are not supposed to command or make our own spirit go into the spirit world or go places beyond our reach. Having the ability to do so through various practices and rituals is ungodly and is witchcraft. I've heard of many Christians with the desire to see the spirit world and to go to those places. They take part in diverse practices that the Lord detests.

There is a movement called the New Age movement that enables you to look into the spiritual world. Many people sadly follow at least one practice of the New Age movement. I will dig deep into the New Age movement and why it is all demonic. I will go into depth on Bible verses towards the end, backing up with scripture all the things that the Lord detests.

A lot of the practices that the New Age is involved in go back to Hinduism and Buddhism. If you're into the New Age, it is all about connecting with your chakras. They believe this allows you to reach a higher consciousness, vibrations of the universe, energies, spiritual healing, and a deeper level of spirituality. I will go over the terminology that comprises this type of movement and what each individual practice is truly invoking into your life.

MUDRA

Mudra is translated as a gesture or seal. Mudras are symbolic hand gestures that are derived from Buddhism. It is the hand gestures you make in relation to the yoga that you are doing. Mudras connect each finger to the five elements: air, water, earth, fire, and space. When you practice mudra with your yoga or meditation, it channels the prana to be within you. Each unique hand pose of mudra has a different purpose.

Photo credit: Laura Juarez

PRANA

Prana is the manifestation of all the energy. They also consider it a life force. Prana is breathing exercises and uses this life force of energy. They used this in many yoga along with certain mudras to bring forth the life force. They call this prana, but in reality, this life force of energy is diabolical and ungodly.

MANTRA

When you are using a mantra in your yoga, this is the repetitive sound that you make when you meditate. It is supposed to penetrate your mind, and the sound vibrations enable you to enter a deep meditation when chanting different mantras. If you break up the word mantra into two words, the word "MAN" means mind and "TRA" means transport or vehicle. A popular mantra is the Om. When you chant the Om mantra, it is pronounced "Aum." There are several mantras, but later on, I will go into detail about this specific mantra and its meaning. Mantras are an invocation to demonic spirits alongside using mudras.

YOGA

They always describe Yoga as this meditative practice to release the stresses of your life. There is plenty of research about the health benefits of yoga that you can find online. The word yoga means union, and originates comes from Hinduism. The culture of Hinduism has a variety of deities or gods. Different poses in yoga summon different demonic spirits. There are many variations of yoga, some involve tranquil music, and others involve chanting or using mudras. Now we have gone over some of the terminology found in this practice. I will also go in-depth into what you are actually taking part in when doing yoga. When you are using mantras and mudras in your everyday life, you are summoning demonic beings into your life. Your participation in Yoga is not as simple and innocent as it first appears. It is not a spiritual energy due to prana; it is not energy of the cosmic that you feel; in reality, it is demons entering your mind and body. You are opening up a doorway for these demons to do as they please, especially if you are calling out to them. This is the specific purpose of using different mantras. It is an act of summoning. This "life force of energy" is a wording that they use to hide the fact that you are conjuring up demonic powers into your life. I will describe only three types of yoga that are very demonic, aside from the entire practice itself.

NAAD YOGA

Naad is defined as the essence of sound. This yoga practice uses different sound vibrations and is also the union of the mind with cosmic consciousness through these sounds. They connect the specific sounds with your mind and with the cosmic.

KUNDALINI YOGA

This type of yoga involves chanting and breathing exercises with repetitiveness. This involves several patterns of singing with chanting when doing Kundalini Yoga. The purpose of this type of yoga is to awaken your energy. They also refer to it as the yoga of awareness. This also brings spiritual enlightenment to your life. Kundalini Yoga uses several mantras to reach spiritual enlightenment.

BHAKTI YOGA

This is known as the devotion yoga and one of the four types of yoga to the path to enlightenment. For Bhakti Yoga, there are nine limbs of devotion.

1. Shravana - Listening to ancient scriptures.
2. Kirtana - Singing devotional songs.
3. Smarana - Remembering the divine.
4. Pada sevana - Practicing and servicing karma yoga (one of the other four types of yoga to enlightenment).
5. Archana - Deity and ritual worship with fire offering.
6. Vandana - Worship, reverence, and praise to Saraswati.
7. Dasya - Devotion to the divine.
8. Sakhya - Relationship between you and the divine.
9. Atma-nivedana - Surrendering to the divine.

PRAVANA YOGA

Pravana means cosmic sound. This yoga aids in meditation. This is the name of a mantra in Hinduism Om. Om is one of the biggest and sacred symbols in Hinduism and this yoga requires you to focus on Om. Om is popular in meditation, chants and prayers in Hindu. Sadly, this is one of the classical forms of mediation that many people do not know what they are even chanting. The Bible tells us to give praises to the Lord and rejoice in his name. Jesus doesn't teach us to chant to Om or to give prayers to Om.

These different yoga, which are only a few out of all that exists, all require you to worship, summon and devote yourself to someone else other than Jesus Christ.

In the book of Matthew, it says you cannot serve two masters. You will either love one or hate the other. This is all demonic and not of God. The Bible teaches us to follow the steps of Jesus. Jesus did not summon and conjure up energies of the cosmic or chant mantras to feel prana. We all must wake up; this is not what the Lord has called us to do!

We are to be renewed of the mind by the Holy Spirit. The Bible teaches us that the Holy Spirit is our comforter, who will show us and teach us all things. We don't need to meditate and chant mantras and do hand mudras. We don't need to be conformed to these idols and gods when the Holy Spirit is here to teach us and convict us! If you devoted all the time that was spent in meditation to reach a "higher consciousness" and instead devoted your time to connecting with the Holy Spirit, your life would drastically change.

Photo credit: Mohamad Hassen

CHAKRA

Chakras are energies within the body and there are seven chakras positioned throughout the body. You can unlock the chakras with meditation, mudras, chanting, and with yoga. I will list all the seven different chakras.

1. Root chakra
2. Sacral chakra
3. Solar plexus chakra
4. Heart chakra
5. Throat chakra
6. Third eye chakra
7. Crown Chakra

I won't go into detail about the specifics of each chakra, but I will talk about the sacral chakra. Supposedly, the specific mantras you chant to unlock this chakra are chants to the god of oceans and creation called

Varuna. This specific chant done to unlock this is called Vam. This mantra chant is summoning a demonic presence into your life. You are worshiping a Hindu goddess in just trying to "unlock your chakra". This is only one of the seven chakras. Imagine how many doors you are opening to the devil by practicing all of your chakras and meditating while chanting to different gods.

We have our minds renewed through the Holy Spirit, not by chakras or energies of the universe. This is deceit from the devil to get you to believe such practices are the way to live out your life. This is the mastermind plan the devil has put throughout the world. By serving these supposed deities and seeking these demonic spirits, we are not serving the one who truly created us, The Lord. We must stop doing this wickedness, repent, and turn to God while there is still time. We are living in the time of mercy and grace and the love of God is never ending. The power and authority of God is infinite. We must not turn to pagan rituals and demonic practices to reach "enlightenment". By doing this, you will not inherit the kingdom of God as it states in Galatians 5.

Titus 3:5-7 (NKJV)

Not by works of righteousness which we have done, but according to His mercy He saved us, through the washing of regeneration and renewing of the Holy Spirit, whom He poured out on us abundantly through Jesus Christ our Savior, that having been justified by His grace we should become heirs according to the hope of eternal life.

BUDDHISM

This tradition believes in enlightenment through meditation. Those who practice this believe in reincarnation. They refer to samsara, which is the cycle of death and rebirth. Buddhism's set of doctrines and disciplines attempt to reach the state of nirvana, to end reincarnation by perceiving eternal truth. In reality, the golden statue of Buddha isn't an object of worship. It is a mere symbolism in their culture of Buddha himself and what he represents. People believe him to have found enlightenment.

Their philosophical traditions have at their core the Four Noble Truths and Noble Eightfold Path. Similar to Christians having the Ten Commandments to follow, The Noble Eightfold Truth is their version of what they consider absolute truths. These truths are supposed to help you reach nirvana and end samsara. Karma is also enormous in this religion; it is the cause and effect of actions. There is a heavy emphasis on meditation along with mantras. During religious ceremonies, Buddhists use prayer wheels and spin the wheels while reciting mantras. They wear prayer beads, also known as mala. These are used to help with meditation while you recite different mantras. These beads count to 108 beads representing the mortal desire you must overcome to reach nirvana according to their beliefs.

Prayer Beads - Photo credit: PRIYA

I needed to explain some background on Buddhism because a lot of the practices in Buddhism have a heavy influence on yoga. Vandana is one of the seven highest ways to worship. Vandana means to worship and praise Saraswati. In Bhakti Yoga, I referenced the nine different devotions required for this yoga. Number six was Vandana, and when you do this type of worship, you are worshiping the Saraswati of the Hindus.

God has been clear in his warning to us. We are not to worship any other gods and to stay away from sorcery. I urge you to throw away any statues from these practices that you may have because that opens doors for demons. The latter parts of the book include more detail on statues and carved items.

Leviticus 26:1 (NKJV)
You shall not make idols for yourselves; neither a carved image nor a sacred pillar shall you rear up for yourselves; nor shall you

set up an engraved stone in your land, to bow down to it; for I am the Lord your God.

HINDUISM

Both Hinduism and Buddhism originated from the ancient cultures of India and share many similarities. In Hinduism, they have a belief that Brahma is the absolute, infinite God. They recognize him as the father of creation, and they consider him the entire existence. Every tradition in Hinduism is rooted in this belief.

This religion believes in reincarnation and the rebirth of souls. The Om mentioned earlier in this chapter is a sacred symbol representing the deity Brahma. When you chant Om in yoga, you are worshiping this infinite god of the Hindus. They worship many deities, and as mentioned above, Saraswati is one of them. She is a Hindu goddess of knowledge and wisdom. They typically represent her as a woman in white sitting on top of a white lotus flower.

The spiritual symbol of Om

MEDITATION

Hinduism and Buddhism place a heavy emphasis on meditation. There are several types of meditation that involve breathing exercises and body movements.

Movement meditation allows you to have a deeper connection with your body. Qi gong and Tai Chi are forms of meditation that are very popular and seen often. As a visual reference, foreign martial arts films use a lot of Tai Chi movements. They believe these movements enhance the balance within your body and they use it for strengthening.

Tai chi originated from Taoism, also called Daoism. Dao means the way. Taoism is the belief in having everything balanced and reinforcing your inner chi to bring good health and longevity. Chi is the force that sets the world and everything into motion. They also considered it the force that sustains everything that is created. Chi and Taoism go hand in hand. Yin Yang is the symbol used in Taoism; it represents a balance in life. Every time you see yin and yang, just remember this is from this belief system that chi is the center of it all.

Yin Yang symbol

Nowhere in this belief does it reinforce the life of Christ. Although this isn't the worst type of meditation out there, by doing this and trying to find your inner chi or force, it is still an act of looking for another substance that isn't Jesus.

Looking at what scripture tells us, it does not reference a chi as a force that sustains all things. It is through and by God himself that everything has been made, not a chi.

Colossians 1:16-17 (KJV)
For by Him all things were created that are in heaven and that are on earth, visible and invisible, whether thrones or dominions or principalities or powers. All things were created through Him and for Him. And He is before all things, and in Him all things consist.

There's also Mantra meditation and spiritual meditation and several others that I won't go into detail about. They both promote and encourage you to connect to a higher power. Spiritual meditation is something you see a lot in Christianity in those who are looking to dive deeper with God. Mantra meditation uses the chanting of the Om as explained earlier in the chapter, and it involves a variety of different chants with the use of hand mudras. Meditating on the Lord isn't a sin. When you involve hand mudras that symbolize other gods, chanting to demons, and trying to invoke energies from the universe, then it becomes something diabolical. Always be very cautious about the information you see on the internet and what you decide to embrace in your everyday living. A lot of what you may perceive to be a harmless thing will open doors for demons to dwell in your life without you even being aware of it.

When you go back into this chapter, you can see where everything originates from and what everything means; it is all diabolical. Nothing that you have read here is what God wants us to practice. None of these teachings is what Jesus did while he was on earth, so in reality who are you serving by doing these practices? We cannot try to live out a life of Christianity while doing these other practices. You are serving two masters. This is what the Bible says about serving two masters.

Matthew 6:24 (KJV)
No man can serve two masters: for either he will hate the one, and love the other; or else he will hold to one, and despise the other. Ye cannot serve God and mammon.

There are so many more practices that are in the New Age I cannot cover here. I will discuss that and much more in the chapters ahead. If you are involved in any of these practices, I pray that the Holy Spirit illuminates and opens up your eyes and your mind to see the darkness that hangs over you, in Jesus' name. Amen.

5

Sorcery

God is the creator of all things in the heavens and on earth. The evils that abide on the earth and in heavenly places are not to be sought after. Evil practices that were mentioned in my previous chapter are an abomination to the Lord. I will continue by unveiling the truths behind these practices.

In the following list are things and practices used to worship the devil and to seek demonic entities.

Seeking energies:

- Vibrations
- Astral projection
- Crystals
- Meditation
- Yoga
- Tarot cards
- Reach higher consciousness
- Physics

- Divination
- Mediums
- Chiromancy
- Gastromancy
- Necromancy
- Astrology
- Angel numbers
- Numerology
- Zodiac signs
- Horoscopes

These practices are ungodly and demonic! The Lord detests every one of these practices. A few of these I have gone over in my last chapter, but I want to dig deeper into other practices. Let's look at what scripture tells us.

Deuteronomy 18:9-12 (NKJV)

When you come into the land which the Lord your God is giving you, you shall not learn to follow the abominations of those nations. There shall not be found among you anyone who makes his son or his daughter pass through the fire, or one who practices witchcraft, or a soothsayer, or one who interprets omens, or a sorcerer, or one who conjures spells, or a medium, or a spiritist, or one who calls up the dead. For all who do these things are an abomination to the Lord, and because of these abominations the Lord your God drives them out from before you.

Galatians 5:19-21 (KJV)

Now the works of the flesh are manifest, which are these; Adultery, fornication, uncleanness, lasciviousness, Idolatry, witchcraft, hatred, variance, emulations, wrath, strife, seditions, heresies, envyings, murders, drunkenness, revellings, and such like: of the which I tell you before, as I have also told you in time past, that they which do such things shall not inherit the kingdom of God.

The Lord detests these abominations, and you must repent and turn your ways to Jesus because summoning demons every day is not the answer. Jesus is.

I will go over some terms that I have listed above.

- **Necromancy** is seeking to summon and obtain information from spirits or the "dead". An example of Necromancy is Tarot cards and Ouija boards.
- **Gastromancy** is predicting the future by gazing into shiny objects or convex mirrors to induce a trance.
- **Divination** is predicting the future by supernatural means which involve fortune telling, chiromancy, tarot cards, and many more.
- In **Numerology** numbers have a hidden meaning and have a spiritual and magical significance.
- **Angel numbers** are spiritual messages in numerology, and it is sequences of patterns and number sequences that hold a spiritual significance.

Astrology is a huge part of the New Age movement. It is also divination that involves observation of the stars, planets, the sun, and moon phases. Astrology looks at the constellations in correlation to your everyday life. They require you to look at your birth chart, zodiac signs, twelve-star constellations, the planets, twelve houses, the sun and moon to predict outcomes in your life. We must not look into horoscopes, for it is the practice of astrology, which is another act of divination. Astrology can take a few years to master and understand because of how complex it is. We only need to understand one thing: Jesus is the way to salvation. That does not require years of understanding; it just takes conviction brought by the Holy Spirit.

Photo Credit: Gordon Johnson

Some people find themselves fixated on finding meaning in their life and finding purpose. The only way to live your life with purpose is with Jesus. Jesus is the way, the truth, and the life. There is no other way to achieve this gratification that is desired, or inner strength that is looked for.

God has everything that you could ever need. He is not like people here that are here one minute and gone the next. He is and always will be an immutable God, which means unchanging. The reason we don't desire God the same way you may desire these other practices is because we are living in the flesh. This flesh wants to sin and wants earthly things, and does not desire God. That is why many people turn to a New Age and traditions like Hinduism and Buddhism. It does not glorify God. Our flesh does not desire the things of God. We are at war with powers and rulers of darkness, as stated in Ephesians 6:12. This evil that servants of the Lord fight against is what you are worshiping when you take part in these customs. Once you open one door of any one of these practices, it is enough to get you involved in the occult.

John 14:6 (NKJV)
Jesus said to him, "I am the way, the truth, and the life. No one comes to the Father except through me."

CRYSTALS

Another thing about the New Age is crystals which are supposed to help aid you in your everyday life. They have healing properties and come in different types and colors which have different significance to them. Very specific crystals, according to the New Age, help with different chakras. Some of these crystals help with the alignment of higher power, such as the ONYX crystal. Crystals are used in yoga and meditation. You can place it anywhere on your being. The deeper you're involved with crystals, the more you learn how to charge them since they contain the energy of the universe. They aid in connecting you with your spirit guides.

Crystals should not be used, especially by Christians! Jesus did not use crystals to help with healing and to help align his energies; this is the work of the devil. For it is in Jesus' name that we are healed from our iniquities and illnesses, not by the work of a "powered crystal." Jesus Christ died on the cross for our transgressions, for our sins and through his stripes, we are healed. Scripture does not insist on us using energy filled crystals when Jesus has already paid the ultimate price for each one of us.

Isaiah 53:5 (NKJV)
But He was wounded for our transgressions, He was bruised for our iniquities; The chastisement for our peace was upon Him, And by His stripes, we are healed.

Spirit guides are something many people, even Christians, are getting confused by. People hear this terminology and associate a spirit guide as being the same thing as the Holy Spirit, because people hear that the Holy Spirit guides you in your life. The Holy Spirit does indeed guide you in your life, but a spirit guide is not the Holy Spirit! This is a demon you are actively communicating with and is very demonic!

Leviticus 19:31 (NKJV)
Give no regard to mediums and familiar spirits; do not seek after them, to be defiled by them: I am the Lord your God.

WITCHCRAFT

The Webster's dictionary defines witchcraft as the use of sorcery or magic, communication with the devil, and rituals and practices that incorporate the belief in magic. Divination is one practice in witchcraft. There are many things in the New Age that are witchcraft. Anything that pertains to divination, which includes tarot cards, gastromancy, necromancy, palmistry, ouija boards, and so much more, is an act of witchcraft. These practices in the New Age are a form of communication with the devil.

Some people may say, I never sold my soul to the devil, so I am not into witchcraft and sorcery. False! You can do any of these evil practices without selling your soul to the devil for rich and fame. If you have not given your life to Jesus Christ and surrendered yourself to him, you belong to a different master. Without Christ, no one can come into the Kingdom of God, and practicing divination is actively serving the devil.

In witchcraft, there is so much more than just divination. Their practices include rituals in the occult and sacrifices that are performed by people that are deeply involved in witchcraft.

A very popular aspect of witchcraft is having the ability to astral project. This practice allows you to travel in the spirit world and results in you controlling your spirit. Many people refer to this as your astral body traveling, but that is, in fact, your actual spirit. Others define this as an out-of-body experience. Astral Projection at will is not of God. We are not called to control our own spirit to go wherever we want it to go. People involved in the occult use this to attack other people or to go some place for whatever reasons they have. This is diabolical and not of God. Many aspects of the New Age help you unlock astral projection by meditation or having you unlock your "Chakras". I didn't specify about this at all in the last chapter because this is much more than enlightenment or having a deeper spiritual sense within yourself. The world tries to mask the real meaning of what you're doing by using these positive words such as getting in touch with the cosmic universe, becoming transcendent, enlightenment, and filling yourself with energies. This is witchcraft, and if you are involved in astral projection, you need to stop and repent to Christ.

Witches and warlocks will often have a "spirit guide" with them, since they are frequently reaching out to demonic forces. They devote so much of their time to worshiping and building altars for Satan. Satan is the father of all lies and only cares to destroy you, as it states in John 8:44.

BLACK MAGIC / WHITE MAGIC

In the occult, they try to categorize the different types of magic. White magic is typically for the act of healing energy, divination, prosperity, blessing a house, or intending to do good. Crystals and chakras go hand in hand with white magic. Black magic is the magic that people do not want to be associated with. They use it with the intent to do harm, for revenge, and to cast spells and curses on people. It doesn't matter what type of "magic" you are using, you are still doing witchcraft and communicating with demonic forces, no matter what the intention is.

Necromancy is also considered black magic to some people because of the rituals behind necromancy. Some people use pentagrams and séances to conjure up the dead. Now, in today's world, we are seeing so many paranormal activity types of shows about people speaking to the "dead". Society has accepted this as perfectly normal and something thrilling to do. Nobody even stops to question anything about what they put on television. They put on their shows different mediums, séances, and they practice talking to the dead. I've even seen another practice with what is called candle magic. On these paranormal shows, I have seen people doing rituals and performing them with candles or gazing into one, hoping to have an encounter with the supernatural. This is all divination, witchcraft and satanic.

This is an act of necromancy. Jesus did not conjure up spirits, so why should we? This is not glorifying God, but giving glory to Satan. We are supposed to follow the ways of Christ. Conjuring up spirits is opening doorways for demons to enter your life. Each act of witchcraft that you do brings in more and more demons and spirits. In these shows, they bring up different herbs and ways to cleanse the houses of those being tormented. This is not biblical and does nothing. The only one who can cleanse your home and your life is God. There are various factors to why a person's home and the atmosphere might be how is it, but I will touch on this later on in the book.

There is also the idea out there that there are good spirits and evil spirits in necromancy. This is a misconception that leads many down this erroneous path. They think they will conjure up good spirits as opposed to evil spirits. There is no such thing as good spirits and evil ones. The only good spirit that you'll find on this earth is called the Holy Spirit. Satan is the father of all lies and this is the biggest lie that people seem to believe across the world. When you are trying to seek the supernatural, you are speaking to demons in whatever form they choose to be in.

Do not be deceived! When you open the doors to spirits and try to communicate with them daily, you are dealing with spiritual wickedness. Whatever spirit guide, or "good spirit" that you think you are talking to, is nothing but evil, and you need to stop and repent. This is what scripture tells us.

Ephesians 6:12 (KJV)

For we wrestle not against flesh and blood, but against principalities, against powers, against the rulers of the darkness of this world, against spiritual wickedness in high places.

SHAMANS

Shamanism, according to Wikipedia, is a religious practice that involves a practitioner (shaman) interacting with what they believe to be a spirit world through altered states of consciousness, such as a trance. According to the Oxford English Dictionary, the word Shaman is someone who is regarded as having access to, and influence in, the world of benevolent and malevolent spirits, who typically enters into a trance state during a ritual, and practices divination and healing.

Shamans are also considered to be witch doctors, healers, sorcerers, or spiritual leaders. Shamans are practicing witchcraft in what they are doing. Do not go to a shaman to be blessed or cured. I urge you not to go to one for a remedy because you are letting someone who does witchcraft empower you with demonic powers. You are allowing doors to be opened to spiritual wickedness in your life. This is very demonic, and nothing good will come from this! This generation needs to wake up and look at what is being done to our nation. We cannot engulf ourselves with wicked things, for those who do them will not enter the Kingdom of heaven. We only need God in our lives to provide us with all that we need. Why seek a sorcerer for your problems? There is no need to infest your lives with demons to heal you, because that's exactly what you are doing by going to a shaman.

Psalms 103:2-4 (NKJV)

Bless the Lord, O my soul, And forget not all His benefits: Who forgives all your iniquities, Who heals all your diseases, Who redeems your life from destruction, Who crowns you with lovingkindness and tender mercies,

Psalms 16:11 (NKJV)

You will show me the path of life; In Your presence is fullness of joy; At Your right hand are pleasures forevermore.

If you knew what you were serving by doing these wicked practices, I guarantee you would not do them. Satan, with his principalities and demons, are horrific beings but yet they are presented as something to be desired. Turn away and repent to Jesus Christ. There is no salvation by worshiping and dedicating your life to Satan and his minions. The only way to life and salvation is through Jesus. I've said this many times and I will continue to say it. God has so much more for your life than you speaking to spirits or being in the supernatural.

There is a power above any power you or Satan may appear to have. God is sovereign, meaning that he has complete control over all things. He rules over all and holds all authority in heaven and on earth. Witches and warlocks think that by worshiping Satan, they gain a power above all other powers. This is the plan of the devil to bind you in your sins and to blind you from the truth. The authority of the *Word* of God is *power* above all other powers over the earth.

John 1:1-5, 10-14 (NKJV)
Philippians 2:8-11 (NKJV)

"In the beginning was the Word, and the Word was with God, and the Word was God. He was in the beginning with God. All things were made through Him, and without Him nothing was made that was made. In Him was life, and the life was the light of men. And the light shines in the darkness, and the darkness did not comprehend it.

He was in the world, and the world was made through Him, and the world did not know Him. He came to His own, and His own did not receive Him. But as many as received Him, to them He gave the right to become children of God, to those who believe in His name: who were born, not of blood, nor of the will of the flesh, nor of the will of man, but of God. And the Word became flesh and dwelt among us, and we beheld His glory, the glory as of the only begotten of the Father, full of grace and truth.

And being found in appearance as a man, He humbled Himself and became obedient to the point of death, even the death of the cross. Therefore God also has highly exalted Him and given Him the name which is above every name, that at the name of Jesus every knee should bow, of those in heaven, and of those on earth, and of those under the earth, and that every tongue should confess that Jesus Christ is Lord, to the glory of God the Father."

6

Fight and Conquer

Into the Mind

Struggles of the mind are more than just bad thoughts coming to your mind; it goes much deeper than that. The devil is a manipulator and a master of the attacks on the mind. In this chapter, I will detail the different methods that the enemy uses to attack our minds in attempts to hinder us.

I want to focus more on a specific attack on the mind. Sometimes your mind becomes blank, empty of all thoughts or knowledge. I've detailed one example from my own life in my last book, so I won't go into my backstory here. I would have strong, heavy mental attacks at random while driving to church or anywhere. In an instant, I would go from being a normal sound-minded person to not remembering what my name was. It sounds bizarre to the average person, but believe me when I say I don't wish this on anyone, not even on my enemies. In an instant I would literally lose grasp of reality, my mind would go blank, and I would know nothing. Everything from what I was doing or where I was going, or even who I was. I didn't know what my existence was for or what created me. These attacks are real and very strong. When I first experienced these attacks, I thought I had lost my mind and thought I was one phone call away to a padded room. I almost emitted myself to be confined to a padded room where crazy people go because I believed I had lost a few marbles and went completely nuts.

Let me tell you something. There was only one word I knew in my vocabulary, in my memory, in my mind, and that was the name Jesus. No matter how strong and evil these demonic attacks were over my life. I would say Jesus, Jesus, Jesus! I would declare his name with the authority given to me from God, and then I would remember the words, "I rebuke you in the name of Jesus". Trust me when I say I only remembered the name of Jesus, just one name. It's the only word that was left inside this head of mine. I would know within myself, "I don't know what my name is, but this name of Jesus has authority and power!" The moment I spoke the name of Jesus, I felt clarity return to my mind once again. It felt like a dark cloud that had been over my mind, blocking everything I knew, had been lifted. I felt like my normal self again, knowing my name and everything else about me. I can't tell you how terrifying it is to experience something to this magnitude, but we can do all things through Christ who strengthens us. If you ever find yourself in any situation like mine, call out the name of Jesus because there is a power of great magnitude and authority in his name. I have other experiences of the mind of which I will not discuss here as I wrote about it in great detail in my previous book.

Try this exercise, declare peace into your mind every day or every week. Say I declare peace in the name of Jesus, I declare peace in my mind, in my home, and everywhere I shall go today. Start declaring peace over your mind if you struggle with attacks like mine. You shall see the power of God manifested in your life, for it says in the bible that God is not the author of confusion and disorder but of peace.

Nightmares

Growing up, I lived in a place that didn't feel normal. There was always a feeling that something malevolent was there. I'm not sure why the place where my family used to live in felt that way, but I suspect it was something that was done to the land many years ago. We used to live in a mobile home on this land. I suffered many nightmares as a child. I always thought that was a very scary place where I felt someone was watching me at all hours. My family has a deep love for the things of God, and we just stepped into a land that had such an ungodly presence over it. The battles began from the moment we started living in this place. I would get nightmares all the time, and it would never stop. As a child, I never knew why they wouldn't stop. I never spoke about it because I never knew someone could have helped me with guidance. Mind you, this place was a place of torment for me. I have no better word to describe the experience there. Most places you live at won't be as horrible as mine unless you live on land where evil has been done to it.

Once I moved out of this place, I remember the first night in our new house. I slept in peace for the first time in years with no fear. If you live in a place that torments you beyond belief, and you need more help than a prayer before sleeping, try anointing your room with oil. If you live in a place that is like where I used to live, I urge you to move and find somewhere else to live. Sometimes the Lord will lead us to do this, and He will open the doors for us to do it. It's not running from the enemy in defeat, but using the wisdom that God tells us to ask for in order to live without perishing. It states in Hosea 4:6 that His people are destroyed for lack of knowledge.

Pray before going to sleep, say this short prayer.

"God, in the name of Jesus, I ask you to protect my mind from evil, and let me rest in peace with no nightmares."

Declare the word of Psalms 4:8 and declare peace over your mind and for protection before sleeping. Pray before going to sleep every night, and you'll be amazed at what one prayer can do in your life.

People always ask where nightmares come from? I did some research on the origins of this word. The word nightmare comes from the old English word for mare. A mare is a mythological demon or goblin that torments with frightening dreams.

We must be careful what we watch or what we do, as it can open doors for evil to come in and cause torment. A long time ago I was watching TV and changing the channels and came across a commercial about a horror movie. I watched only 10 seconds of this commercial and without putting more thought into it. I went to bed much later, and I had a nightmare, waking up in sweats, because of this commercial. Malevolent spirits cause nightmares. God is a god of peace, not someone who brings terror into your life. Nightmares do not come from God. They come from what we do in our everyday life. What we watch right before bed can influence how we sleep. If we watch horror movie after horror movie before going to bed, we can allow doors to be opened resulting in spiritual attacks. Not everything with the title of it being a horror movie is going to cause an attack. I simply urge you to be careful of what you watch. Stay away from TV shows or movies that have a séance in them, and incantations of tongues because you don't know what those tongues are saying or summoning.

Often, people think monsters might be a figment of your imagination because of how often little children speak of monsters being in the closet. You've heard of all of those stories from children of a monster being under their bed. Many parents dismiss this as being a child's imagination.

Children are more susceptible to seeing spiritual wickedness and evil around us. They are still developing and learning right from wrong. As young children, they haven't formed strong biases of anything like adults have, and they are just accepting of what we teach to them. Children are being attacked at such an early age and demons present themselves to these kids as their friends. Children will accept this form of communication with their "friend" unbeknownst to them of what they are actually talking to. By being presented with such a demonic encounter after encounter, kids will not know any different. They'll grow up learning to speak to spirits. They will open the door to so many things by inviting evil spirits into the home and their lives. That results in teens growing up with problems. It will manifest in their attitude, character, drugs, and many other things that God does not want for our children.

It's sad that there aren't enough vigilant parents looking out for their kids. We dismiss these alarming things our children try to tell us, and when they grow up, we wonder why they have so many problems. Parents, teach your kids who Jesus is and teach them to pray. Help them build a foundation on the word of God. Teach them what is good and righteous. Teach them to love the things of God and to rebuke evil.

Sleep Paralysis

I also want to bring to your attention sleep paralysis. Science and the medical doctors describe this as someone who experiences the feeling of being awake but cannot move or speak. Everyone has heard of this terminology and has concluded that it's medical and has a scientific explanation. I've heard of testimonies from people still calling it this, but in reality, it is a demonic attack. The feeling of not being able to move or speak is a demon attacking you in the form of a paralysis. People nowadays call it sleep paralysis, but do not be confused or believe the lie. I've even heard people consider sleep paralysis to cause hallucinations of evil. There is nothing hallucinative about seeing spirits. You are being attacked. Don't consume sleeping pills or medicine to fight off the devil. The enemy can only be conquered through the authority that Jesus Christ has given you. It is easy to forget that the devil and his demons have their own power. Thinking that they have no power at all is naïve. It will cause us to perish. The Bible tells us that greater is He (Jesus) that is in us than he that is in the world. There is no other name above the name of Jesus. Speak the name of Jesus and all evil must flee! Even if you cannot speak the name Jesus with your voice, say it in your mind and rebuke to fight off this attack. There is power in what we proclaim and declare. There is power in the name of Jesus.

Objects / Statues

If you are being tormented day in and day out, ask yourself this: did you let these spirits into your life that are tormenting you? How many of us have received gifts from people unknowing where these gifts came from? How many of us who have received gifts given by people then go to display these gifts afterward? You must look around your house at all the things you have inside. Look for idols and statues of creatures or anything that looks to be an idol. If you have a statue of a demon or anything that represents something diabolic, you are allowing malevolent spirits to enter your home. By having this statue, for example, you are opening up a doorway for these demons to enter your life and cause torment. Let's just say that you aren't even worshiping this statue in your home, but by having it, you are still allowing evil to roam around and do as they please.

When you go over to a friend's house, what is the first thing you do? Of course, you say hi and make it known that you have arrived at your friend's home. You then make yourself comfortable, grab a beverage or snack and enjoy your stay. What makes you think if you open a door to a demon that this entity will not do the same? Do you think this evil presence in your home will just stay quiet or go away on its own? It won't leave as long as it's welcomed there.

First, you might have trouble with your finances, then your marriage, and then it goes on from there. We must cleanse our homes from idols, statues, or anything that worships an image. This also doesn't just pertain to statues, but objects that have been made unholy.

For instance, one day my mother came home with something she picked up from the side of the road. As soon as she brought that object into the home, I believe it to have been a blanket of some sort. When it entered my home, my pans began moving on their own. I was trying to make breakfast, so it annoyed me I couldn't make my breakfast. The pots and pans moving around on the kitchen stove top didn't scare me, but I looked around at what had just changed to cause this disturbance. I saw my mom arriving home happy bringing in whatever she found outside. I remember asking her if she had just brought anything home. After she told me what it was, I told her to throw it away as I wanted to finish making breakfast and couldn't because the pans wouldn't stop moving. I say this very nonchalant, but that is because occurrences like these are nothing to me, but I still have to be vigilant.

God detests the worshiping of other idols or anything of this earth. Throw out your carved items that are unholy and doing this will cleanse your home. As discussed in the New Age chapter, I explained in great detail the significance of the Hindu and Buddhist religions. Especially the statues that go along with these two cultures and what their gods are. Hinduism, as I explained in earlier chapters, has many deities that are worshiped, and I have given a description of one of them. Be cautious of what you buy and bring into your home because God detests idols. You will see more peace and clarity in your home if you clear out these idols and carved images that you may have.

Bible verses to reflect on from this chapter.

Leviticus 26:1

You shall not make idols for yourselves; neither a carved image nor a sacred pillar shall you rear up for yourselves; nor shall you set up an engraved stone in your land, to bow down to it; for I am the Lord your God.

Exodus 20:4-5 (NKJV)

You shall not make for yourself a carved image any likeness of anything that is in heaven above, or that is in the earth beneath, or that is in the water under the earth,

you shall not bow down to them nor serve them. For I, the Lord your God, am a jealous God, visiting the iniquity of the fathers upon the children to the third and fourth generations of those who hate Me.

Isaiah 42:8 (NKJV)

I am the Lord, that is My name; And My glory I will not give to another, Nor My praise to carved images.

James 1:5 (NKJV)

If any of you lacks wisdom, let him ask of God, who gives to all liberally and without reproach, and it will be given to him.

Philippians 4:13 (KJV)

I can do all things through Christ which strengtheneth me.
Proverbs 22:6 (KJV)

Train up a child in the way he should go: and when he is old, he will not depart from it.

1 Corinthians 14:33 (NIV)

For God is not a God of disorder but of peace as in all the congregations of the Lord's people.

7

Suicide

The devil has such a powerful hold over our nation. We must not give in to his tactics, men, women, and youth. Before your ministry and your purpose can take off, he will try to destroy you. One way he does that is by trying to get you to suicide.

It is a deep, saddening reality that our youth, children, and even older men and women are taking their lives at an instant. According to the CDC website, it states that 45,979 people have died by suicide in the year of 2020. According to the study done in the same year, people over the age of 85 had the higher rates of suicide. Firearms, overall, were used in over 50% of all suicides. 26% of suicides were caused by suffocation. According to the save.org statistics, in 2020, suicide is the 12th leading cause of death. According to the Suicide Awareness Voices of Education, in America alone, you have 125 people die by this every single day. Every 27.5 seconds, someone attempts suicide. They have conducted these studies here in our country. They are specific to America, not globally. Among those 15 to 24 years old, suicide is the 3rd leading cause of death in America.

These numbers and facts are alarming. It should cause a stirring within your soul to want to reach out with love and compassion to those who need it. People wake up, our nation is dying at its own hands! We must go out and fight against this. I overcame this through the power of Christ. I shall recount my experience to you all because I truly understand and sympathize with the suffering one goes through in depression.

Throughout my journey, I entered a heavy state of depression. My partner and I were going to get married, but God had other plans. It all ended with peace between him and me, but it almost destroyed me. We had nearly paid for everything and this experience was very painful. The thought of having everything and nothing from one second to the next ate away at my soul. It brought me into this never-ending loop of depression.

Every day, I would wake up feeling nauseous at the thought of food or the smell of food. In the beginning, I lost my appetite for a little over a week. I was losing one pound a day, which was not healthy, considering I wasn't even eating by this point. I only ate 10% of the food I had on my plate during those painful days. It was 10 days of horrible nausea at the sight of food. Now everyone who knows me knows I am a huge foodie at heart. The thought of hating food disgusted me. Afterward, I began eating a full breakfast, which was better than not eating.

This brought a new level of depression within me, which I never knew existed. This overwhelming feeling of being a failure came and took its place. I would sulk in my bed and cry myself to sleep every night. In my prayers, I would cry out to God, begging for him to remove this feeling of despair. I asked him to let it end because I couldn't bear it. The hopelessness I felt was overwhelming. I struggled to sleep because of how puffed up my face had been because of all the crying. It was a process that I had to get through.

I couldn't deal with this immense feeling of having no hope at all, and before I knew it, suicidal thoughts started creeping in. The thought grew so much in me that I didn't know what to do with myself.

I remember saying to myself, this must be how people without God feel right before they commit suicide. This is the last feeling they will ever feel on this physical earth before ending their lives. Can it be possible that despair and hopelessness are the last things that flow within their hearts? For them, living life is so excruciating. They cannot find peace and comfort in anything anymore. They cannot bear the thought of living another second. How did I get to this point where I sit here in my bed having this urge to end my life? I know what this is now. I can comprehend what people of this world feel before they end their lives. Their pain is real, and they see death as the only hope. People can't understand what it feels like until you are in that position of despair to that severity.

Breathing in the air hurt my soul. The thought of continuing with life felt like being condemned to a lifetime of pain. Smiling at people disturbed me, knowing that I felt like a decaying corpse on the inside. Sorrow consumed me. I know who I am in Christ, but that wasn't enough to rid me of the emotions that followed me everywhere I went. How I longed for relief, even if it was for a few moments. I always thought to myself, I cannot allow myself to feel this weak and fragile when I am supposed to be this strong warrior in Christ. I couldn't understand how I could have these types of thoughts and struggles after being freed from everything else I went through.

There was no relief when I went to church; I felt the same as I did at home. Nobody knew how badly I was suffering. I was too terrified to reach out to anybody because of what people may think or say. I thought talking to someone would not do me any good. One day during this pain, I wanted to go to Walmart and buy a big bottle of pills and consume it with bleach to end my life. I went to the store, parked in the parking lot, and stood there for about 20 minutes, staring into space. I said to myself, today isn't the day to do this, perhaps next week, and on my way back home I felt this feeling of peace rush over my body out of nowhere. Peace came over me, surrounding me as I'd never felt it before. That was God hovering over me at that moment, and I went home in peace.

1 Corinthians 14:33
God is not a God of confusion and disorder but of peace.

I prayed to God, saying that I didn't want to feel this way anymore. Help me, Lord! The following Sunday, I went to church, and the preacher made an altar call after the preaching had finished. My mother actually grabbed me to lead me up to the altar during the altar call. Mothers, I tell you, do not hesitate when God moves you to act! During this, someone came to me praying in tongues, and she put her hand over my heart. God used her to minister to me. God spoke to me, saying that I was going through a transition. He healed my heart that day and with that act of healing, I was able to rise up again and continue on in the walk of the Lord.

Psalm 121:1

I lift up my eyes to the hills. Where does my help come from?
My help comes from the LORD, the Maker of heaven and earth.

Everything was returning almost back to normal in my life. These horrible thoughts of suicide went away with my last encounter with it. God healed me of this pain that had consumed me. I began going out to eat because that brings me joy.

Right now I still am going through what I call the season of loneliness. This season which I find myself in is horrible. We always talk about what Christians go through in everyday living, but what does it mean to be lonely? I couldn't understand why this year had been so hard. Through it all, God kept on moving me to write about how I am feeling in my loneliness. Over and over, God kept on telling me to write. I always questioned it. Why would I want to write about this dreadful feeling of loneliness? The answer is quite simple. I'm not the only person on this earth feeling so low and sunken. As I continued going to church, I kept feeling not seen or heard, just forgotten. I felt like I was everybody's second thought and never anyone's priority. I felt for months and months such forsakenness. Feeling forsaken by everybody is a horrible feeling to experience day in and day out. It's difficult to believe in blessings and for brighter days to come. At one point, people weren't even talking to me. Perhaps it was the seasons and holidays being around the corner, but I was left alone for several months.

I know why I needed to write about this. Somebody needed to hear that there is someone out there who feels the same as you do. Whoever you are that needs to read this, you are not alone. Satan is a liar, and he is the father of all lies. I rebuke the lies and deceit in the name of Jesus.

It's such a terrible stigma to think that we aren't supposed to fail or fall in the works of the Lord. We are not called to be perfect, and we will fail because we are human. We all fall short of the glory of God. It's easy to think to yourself what people would say or think of me if people knew how low I truly felt. How would I be looked at? Would I be seen as someone who's strong or someone who is weak? That haunted my inner thoughts for quite some time. We don't say enough to the future and growing generation that it is ok to be weak; it is ok to fall. It's in our weakness that God glorifies himself in us, and he does not abandon us there. He goes into the pit with us, his presence surrounds us even more when we are at our weakest. Imagine what the power of God can do in our lives during our most fragile state.

I invite you to ask this in a short prayer. Say "God show me who you are." He will show you who he is and more in Jesus' name. Be prepared for what you ask for because He will reveal himself to you. Be prepared to be changed, moved, and convicted by the Holy Spirit. Prepare to be sought out with this everlasting love that you have never experienced before. When we least expect it, God reveals himself to us in his perfect timing.

Everyone has their own path to follow. This has been my experience with depression and with God. Sometimes we go through prolonged periods of time in our situations and circumstances and our bodies adapt. Our physical brain and body begin to function differently. Sometimes we need help to get out of it. You should not feel ashamed if you need help.

There are tools at our disposal provided to help people with mental stability. There is depression medication, anxiety medication, and even therapy that can help. If you have clinical depression, a more severe form of depression, it needs to be treated to help the brain function how it is supposed to. I encourage you to talk to a physician to help take you in the right direction. I say this with encouragement and compassion. We all need to recognize when it is time to seek help on this serious topic of suicide and depression. I strongly encourage you to keep taking your medication if your doctor has determined you need it. In addition to this, we must start to build a relationship with Jesus and surround ourselves with godly people while in this process. Surrounding yourself with people that have the light of Jesus will only push you towards a God-centered life. The Bible tells us that as iron sharpens iron, so a man sharpens the countenance of his friends. Imagine being around drug addicts and being in such a depressed state of mind. You need to surround yourself with people that will speak life into your life! I am a true believer in speaking life into your surroundings and to the people that dwell with you. There is power over what you speak, and the words that come out of your mouth. Begin your day by speaking words of life every morning over yourself. Do not be discouraged if you do not see results right away. Keep a strong faith and keep declaring the words of life. Do not start the day by bashing your life before you can even get out of bed.

Fear not of the statistics in this chapter because we have a God who can prevail amid our troubles. In the name of Jesus, we can break the chains that the enemy tries to bind us with. When you feel like there is something in your life holding you back from what God has for you, that is a stronghold on your life. It is very easy to open doors for demons to come into our lives, especially when we are young and without experience. It's easier to open these doors unknowingly than it is to realize what these doors are in order to close them in Jesus' name. If you are in a place where you have no direction and no one to turn to, the Lord is a strong tower for the oppressed. He is a refuge in times of trouble. Cry to him. He will incline his ear to your call. If you find yourself amongst any of the statistics above and are in a time of trouble, reach out to a godly person full of the Holy Spirit! Find someone to talk to if possible because the only substance to this life of ours comes from the Father, Son, and the Holy Spirit.

When people are experiencing times of oppression and depression, or going through suicidal moments, it's hard to find the strength or courage to speak out to someone for help. I know because I've been there. You have this suffocating feeling of darkness surrounding your every move, feeling like you can't speak to people for guidance. Going through this moment of self-harm feels like an infection radiating your body like an illness. Filling every pore with lies, self-defeat, or even regret. I know how it feels to think of yourself as something less significant than the dirt beneath your feet, and that it's unbearable to live with each gasp of air that you take. The pain we carry can be so unbearable that we think suicide is the only answer. What you really want is relief from your pain. That is why people end up taking their own lives. Just know that I 100% understand you. I come to tell you that you are not alone in this world. You have a purpose to live for, to fight for, and to breathe for. If you were born on this earth, it is for a purpose. God is here with open arms.

Many people say why doesn't just God take my problems away, why did God allow tragedy to hit my life and take away the only person I've ever loved? Or they say if God was real, why did I deserve to suffer when he is God with all the power? These are real thoughts and questions people have. We all have questioned the unknown and what we don't understand. Suffering is part of this life that we live. God is not to be blamed for your circumstance or tragedies. We all reap what we sow. A lot of circumstances that happen on this earth are created by us and could have been prevented. Other circumstances are just meant to be and only God knows the purposes of all things.

You have a purpose on this earth, and we are called to seek God and his righteousness, just as Jesus did when he was on earth. There is a reason you exist. If you ask God to show you who he is and why you're here, he will answer you. God is a gentleman, and he will wait for you to seek him and ask him for the desires your heart. God is here to comfort you in your distress. He is a God who heals and draws near to the brokenhearted. As we go through life, we go through different seasons, as stated in Ecclesiastes chapter three. There is a time for and a season for every purpose here on earth.

When I walked through this valley of depression it was overwhelming. I couldn't even look anybody in the eye or have conversations with people. That was no way of living. When depression hits, it does not come from God. It states in Corinthians 14:33 that God is not a God of confusion or disorder but of peace. God is a God of peace, not a God of depression and because of that, we can overcome this through Jesus' name. The spirit of depression tries to latch deep into your life by hindering every little thing that you do, but there is more power in the name of Jesus. God has more authority over everything that creeps on the earth. He reigns and is above all things above and below the earth.

It says in the bible where the spirit of the Lord is, there is freedom. If you are someone struggling with these things that I have mentioned and are walking in the path of God, you must not forget about the Holy Spirit. The Holy Spirit is here to guide us and to be with us wherever we go.

I encourage you to open your mouth and declare this prayer aloud: I rebuke the demon of depression and suicide and cast it out in the name of Jesus. Demons that torment my mind and spirit, I command you to leave in the name of Jesus. I declare that every door you come from will be closed. There is no other name above the name of Jesus (Philippians 2:9-10). In God is my salvation and my glory; The rock of my strength, And my refuge, is in God (Psalms 62:7). I declare peace over my mind, body, and soul, in Jesus' name. Amen.

I urge anyone that doesn't have anyone to reach to go to save.org. They have tools and support to help you or someone that you may know in dark times. Suicide and depression aren't what people ask for when they wake up in the morning. There are people willing to listen to you and give you the resources that you may need in your time of sorrow and despair.

Never forget about God because we are living in dark times, and we need to draw as close as we can to the never-ending love that God provides. Start building a relationship with the almighty God. All you have to do is open up your heart to him and be willing to let him in.

2 Corinthians 3:17 (KJV)
Now the Lord is that Spirit: and where the Spirit of the Lord is, there is liberty.

Proverbs 18:21 (NIV)
The tongue has the power of life and death, and those who love it will eat its fruit.

Proverbs 18:10 (NKJV)
The name of the Lord is a strong tower: the righteous run into it,

and is safe.

Psalms 9:9 (KJV)
The Lord also will be a refuge for the oppressed, a refuge in the times of trouble.

Proverbs 24:16 (NKJV)
For a righteous man may fall seven times and rise again, But the wicked shall fall by calamity.

Romans 3:23 (NKJV)
For all have sinned and fall short of the glory of God.

John 8:44 (NKJV)
You are of your father the devil, and the desires of your father you want to do. He was a murderer from the beginning, and does not stand in the truth, because there is no truth in him. When he speaks a lie, he speaks from his own resources, for he is a liar and the father of it.

8

Authority

As you work towards the calling that God has over your life, you must equip yourself with the full armor of God, as stated in the book of Ephesians. The part of the armor that I want to focus on is the sword of the spirit. Many people always talk about the other parts of the armor of God, but what is the sword of the spirit? It is the word of God. The Bible is more than just a bunch of words written on a page; it has life, authority and power because the word *is* God. It says in the Bible that he has made my mouth like a sharp sword. We must use the word of God to pierce through evil that confronts us. Piercing through any spirit and spiritual wickedness. The word of God is a tool to use in our everyday life, but it's also a weapon to fight against the darkness of this world. It says in the Bible that he has given us the power to tread on serpents, scorpions, and against all the power of the enemy. God gave us authority when we accepted Christ. The Bible teaches us to be Christ-like, but how do you think we can be like Christ having no authority? We cannot.

Luke 10:19 (KJV)

Behold, I give unto you power to tread on serpents and scorpions, and over all the power of the enemy: and nothing shall by any means hurt you.

Hebrews 4:12 (KJV)
For the word of God is quick, and powerful, and sharper than any two-edged sword, piercing even to the dividing asunder of soul and spirit, and of the joints and marrow, and is a discerner of the thoughts and intents of the heart.

Let's look at the Webster dictionary on the word authority. The word authority means the legal or rightful power; a right to command or to act. This is the definition, but what does this mean for us? Jesus has paid the price for all of us. Because of this, when we receive salvation, He gives us authority over the evil that reigns on the earth. God gave you the right and rightful power to conquer the evil in this world. It's amazing to realize this, and yet we still see God's people struggle every day, not knowing what they hold.

As followers of Christ, you receive authority to trample and defeat the wickedness of this world and its power because their power is nothing compared to the power of God. People make the mistake of thinking the enemy has no power because they think: we have Christ and there is no other greater authority than the power of Christ. But the devil has power, and if we don't know how to use our spiritual weapons and authority, we cannot conquer evil. I encourage you to dive into the word of God because the sword of the spirit is God's word. We all must start learning to study his word. If you don't know how, now there is so much technology at your disposal to learn. If we are all going to be on social media, use it to feed your spirit with knowledge of God's word.

Imagine having a stainless steel sword forged and crafted by a swordsmith. Imagine how confident you feel as you hold its weight in your hands. Hear the sound it makes, how it rings with power as you wield it. If I were in immediate danger, and if all I had was that sword, I wouldn't hesitate to use it. It's difficult for some to believe that words can be as powerful as a sword in your palm. It's hard to understand the concept that the word of God is the sword of the spirit. When we verbally declare Bible verses, that word of God can and will make something happen.

Isaiah 55:11 tells us, *So shall My word be that goes forth from My mouth; It shall not return to Me void, But it shall accomplish what I please, And it shall prosper in the thing for which I sent it.*

A shift has to occur when we declare His word in our lives. Change will manifest when we use the word that is living and powerful. A sword is an inanimate object because it is not a living thing. It is only a weapon that on its own has no power. The word of God is life; it is power. After a certain time, metals can break down and weaken, causing a sword to break, but God's word is everlasting. The Bible, the word of God, is sharper than any sword and will pierce through spirit. You must learn to change the way you think about what the Bible is. It's not just words on a page, it is a weapon and a power that is very much a necessity in spiritual warfare. Changing your perspective will cause a reaction and this reaction will bring a supernatural change in your life. You will see yourself grow in the Lord and will deepen your relationship with him.

You and I have the power to defeat evil. We must rebuke in the name of Jesus. There are demons who have little power and there are others that have a higher power to them. Therefore, some require more intensive fasting and prayer to remove it. Below are two different verses I will talk about regarding this.

In the Bible, in Matthew 17:14-21, the disciples could not rebuke a demon that was inside a child, and they brought this child to Jesus. Within that very hour, Jesus rebuked the demon. The disciples later asked him why they could not cast out the demon. Jesus responded because of their disbelief they could not cast this demon out. He also tells them this demon can only be cast out by prayer and fasting. Even though we have been given power, we cannot just rebuke demons out of anyone without being steadfast in prayer and fasting.

Mark 19:14-29 also depicts a similar story of a possessed child not being able to be liberated by the disciples. When we take the sword of the spirit and use it while casting out demons, we must be in prayer and communion with God. Anyone can recite scripture, but not everyone believes, and your disbelief will hinder miracles, and cause you to fail, just like the disciples did in these verses. You can not act on authority and not believe. You must believe and have faith in what you are proclaiming or doing in order to accomplish anything involving spiritual warfare.

Anything that isn't peace is not from God. When we feel depressed, it is a sign to rebuke depression in the name of Jesus, and demons will have to flee. There is no name greater than the name of Jesus. Every other name is below Jesus and has no power over him. There is no reason to suffer in this way when God offers us peace. We need to learn to apply his word in our lives and use the power he has placed in our hands.

Besides knowing and using the word of God during your spiritual attacks, there are several other tactics in conquering evil. In dark times, when it is needed, you may also anoint your home with oil. Typically, this is done with oil that someone or yourself has prayed for. In a lot of church events, I used to see gift baggies being handed out with a little bottle of anointed oil. I will never forget those days. I would always carry those little plastic bottles of anointed oil with me everywhere I went, just in case I needed it.

You must anoint their house or room if you are being heavily attacked by malevolent spirits. Or if you are being put into fear of having so many attacks. When using oil to anoint your home, apply it to every window opening, every entrance, and all the different walls in the room. You don't have to dredge your walls with oil; just simply tap your walls with your finger that has the oil on it. While anointing, say a prayer and if you are lost in what you should say, I will write out a prayer for any situation when anointing a room or a house.

As you are anointing your room or house, say this prayer aloud.

I anoint this room in the name of Jesus. God, I ask that your presence dwells in this place. I ask that you take out anything that is not of you and I rebuke anything that does not belong and that prevents your presence from entering. I anoint the walls and ask for your protection over this place. I ask for your angels to surround this area and to help me fight what I cannot see with my own physical eyes. I declare peace over this room and peace when I lay down to sleep at night in Jesus' name. Amen.

In my last book, Breaking Free, I talk in great detail about my experiences. For a long time, I was anointing my room often. I can tell you from experience that anointing your home or room works. As I stated in previous chapters, if you have idols, statues, and any perverse things in your home, you will need to do some cleaning first.

I've even heard of Christian teachers in public schools anointing their own classroom they teach in. You may say, why is that, if it's a public place with hundreds of different kids wandering around? The answer is simple: there is so much evil hindering the young people, especially in school. Imagine having one room that you always felt peace in for unknown reasons amid all the chaos. I have had this experience myself and can tell you when I walked into my high school teacher's biology class there was this peace overflowing the classroom. At first, I didn't pay attention to the atmosphere, but as school went on I remember feeling different only inside this specific classroom. This teacher wasn't just any teacher, she was a Christian and God resided in her. I can't remember or have any knowledge if she ever anointed her room, but I can tell you that God's presence was in that room at all times. Just being in that room made an impact on my day. Imagine how many other kids have been blessed as well.

A lot of times in our daily lives, we don't notice when problems begin in our homes until it snowballs into something much bigger. I've heard of many testimonies about this very thing. We all know of the verse, ask and you shall receive. Let's start asking God to unveil the wrong doings in our life. There may just be things in your garage or left behind somewhere that should not be in your home without you even realizing it. Especially if you have kids, since kids and teenagers do a lot without your knowledge. Always ask God to illuminate your mind and to reveal things in your life or house that God does not approve of. If you ask, God will listen and he will respond.

Bible verses to reflect on this chapter:

John 1:1 (KJV)

In the beginning was the Word, and the Word was with God, and the Word was God.

Ephesians 6:12 (KJV)

For we do not wrestle against flesh and blood, but against principalities, against powers, against the rulers of the darkness of this age, against spiritual hosts of wickedness in the heavenly places.

Ephesians 6:13-17 (KJV)

Therefore take up the whole armor of God, that you may be able to withstand in the evil day, and having done all, to stand. Stand therefore, having girded your waist with truth, having put on the breastplate of righteousness, and having shod your feet with the preparation of the gospel of peace; above all, taking the shield of faith with which you will be able to quench all the fiery darts of the wicked one. And take the helmet of salvation, and the sword of the Spirit, which is the word of God;

Isaiah 49:2 (KJV)

And he hath made my mouth like a sharp sword; in the shadow of his hand hath he hid me, and made me a polished shaft; in his quiver hath he hid me;

1 Peter 5:8 (KJV)

Be sober, be vigilant; because your adversary the devil, as a roaring lion, walketh about, seeking whom he may devour.

9

Faithful God

Chains Break

Bondage, strongholds, and burdens are all words used to describe someone who lives with some sort of captivity in their life. Jesus sets us free, but our habits and lifestyles do not change from one minute to the next. When he brings healing into our lives, we see immediate change. Most times, however, change is a gradual process that is more like our natural physical growth. When we come to Christ, we are reborn and made new. As life continues, we tend to not pay attention to the things that still hinder us in our lives. Many people, even God's people, have deep roots of bondage and need to be freed.

We must be careful what we watch and what we look at. Everything we set our eyes on, we allow into our hearts and minds. The Bible references our eye as the lamp of the body and if we corrupt ourselves with our eyes, then our whole body shall be full of darkness. We put ourselves into bondage without it being intentional, and over time, this

73

grows into strongholds that are hard to break. Studying God's word is so vital for us to have knowledge of how to live a life without corruption. We are the light of the world. We cannot mesh the works of God with the darkness of the world. Don't corrupt yourself by partaking in worldly attributes.

Continuous sin will keep spiritual chains on us and keep spiritual doors open for the enemy. Sin clashes with what the Holy Spirit is doing in our lives. Since our body is the temple of the Holy Spirit, we cannot continue to sin and expect God to free us from our bondage. We must not walk after the flesh, but walk after the spirit. Ever wonder what this means? It says in the book of Romans that the carnal mind is in enmity against God. Enmity is a word that means hostility, ill will, and hatred. The carnal mind hates and opposes the holiness of God, and it will bring you to your spiritual death. Having a spiritual mind allows you to have life and peace.

>*Romans 8:6 (NKJV)*
>
>*For to be carnally minded is death, but to be spiritually minded is life and peace.*
>
>*Romans 8:7 (KJV)*
>
>*Because the carnal mind is enmity against God: for it is not subject to the law of God, neither indeed can be.*

When we are bound with spiritual chains, we are in captivity. The Bible references people in captivity as prisoners. This captivity is a concept that people find hard to understand. So much of this generation suffers with affliction and torment. They struggle against strongholds and pull against their chains, but they cannot break free. In desperation, they bang their heads against the wall until they bleed thinking if they harm themselves their captors will release them, but it only makes them laugh. They feel hopeless. The result of this leads many people to end their lives or throw it away. Jesus came to bring salvation. He came to set you free. Call upon the Lord, and he will come to your aid. His timing is always perfect, but his will is not our will. Our thoughts are not his thoughts, and we must understand that being in his absolute perfect will, can and will conflict with our own mindset. Maybe there is a secret sin in your life that you fight against every day but can't ever seem to overcome. Perhaps you were abused, perhaps molested. Maybe there are demonic doorways in your life that you left wide open. You need to seek deliverance from the Lord.

The authority behind the name of Jesus is much more powerful than you and I can comprehend.

In the book of Acts chapter 16, it describes when Paul and Silas went to prison. Even though they had been whipped and were chained up in prison, they started praying and singing hymns of God. Everyone could hear them and this caused an earthquake. The Bible tells us that the foundations of the prison were shaken. Every single prison door was opened and everyone's chains were loosened. Their prayer and worship didn't just cause liberation for just themselves, everybody's chains were loosed. When we go deep into prayer and bring worship to the Lord, something has to change. The atmosphere has to change, your situation has to be shifted.

We should not forget about the Holy Spirit. He gives us understanding and wisdom the deeper we are in the things of God. The Holy Spirit is here to convict us and draw us closer to God. He is our comforter and is here with us every day to help with our infirmities, as it states in

Romans 8:26. Where the spirit of the lord is, there is freedom. We need to learn to pray and fast to break certain strongholds. As we draw closer to God, he will close doors we opened when we were in the world. He will cleanse us from the inside out through the work of the Holy Spirit.

In our situation, we need to keep worshiping God and proclaiming a change. If prayer and worship had no effect, then Paul and Silas would have never been set free. We have to praise him in the middle of our circumstance, in the middle of our sorrow, in the middle of our affliction. When we worship him, we have to worship in spirit and in truth. Provoking the presence of God to move is such a beautiful thing to witness and feel. You don't need to be in the presence of a fancy evangelist to provoke the presence of God to move. In the book of Matthew 18:20, it says where there are two or three gathered in my name; I am there.

Faith

In the book of 1 Peter 1:7, it speaks about our faith being more precious than gold and being tested by fire to glorify God. Our faith will be tested in order for us to grow in God. The Bible describes Abraham as a man of God, a man of faith. He, without question, was in total obedience to God in everything God asked of him. Abraham's faith was tested when God asked him to offer his only son as an offering on a mountain. He built an altar, preparing it for the offering to God in obedience. Just as he was about to kill his son as an offering, an angel called out his name. He told him not to lay a hand on Isaac for he knows Abraham fears God. We know Abraham as the father of faith, however, Jesus is described as the author and perfecter of our faith. In Hebrews 11:1, it says that faith is the substance of things hoped for, the evidence of things not seen. We also cannot please God without having faith, for we must believe that he is and always will be God. We cannot believe and have faith while we doubt. The Bible describes the person who doubts as a wave of the sea being tossed by the wind.

In Psalms 107, it says to cry out to the Lord, and he will save you from your distress. He will bring you out of your darkness and break your chains. When we cry out to the Lord, we must act in faith while doing so. Faith without works is dead and works without faith are also dead. We cannot have one without incorporating the other. In Luke 8:43-48 and Mark 5:25-34, it talks about the woman who had the issue of blood for twelve years. She had tried to be healed by doctors, but none could help her. When she saw Jesus pass by, she knew she had to fight for her miracle. Despite there being so many people surrounding Jesus, she went through the multitude, acting in faith. She touched the border of Jesus' garments, and instantly she was healed. Jesus felt power leave his body when someone touched him and questioned the multitude. The woman came forth. Jesus said that her faith had made her whole and to go in peace. The act of faith and doing something about it caused a miracle in her life and brought Glory to God through her act of faith. His power brought forth healing in her body and that sickness that hindered her for so long, ceased in an instant when she acted in her faith. It wasn't because the garment had special healing powers; it was her faith.

Here in my room as I was talking to God, I was reminded of a time in my life when I had come back to Christ. I won't go into full details on my return to Christ. You can reference my full testimony in my previous book. During this, I had moved back in with my parents with the clothes that I had on my back in the literal sense. I was in a dark place; I was in danger, and my faith caused a shift in my situation. My faith prompted

God to open doors and move me back home to my safety. During the move, I had only about two pairs of clothes that I brought back with me. When I moved back home, it was the most difficult and trying time of my life. I hadn't brought back hardly any clothes, suddenly I had various women of God in my parents' church bring me bags of clothes. When I say bags of clothes, I am not talking about a supermarket bag. I am speaking about those big black hefty types of bags that you use for big garbage. It wasn't just one big bag filled with clothes; it was several big black bags filled with clothes, dresses, shoes; you name it. It was such an abundance of clothes that I couldn't even fit them in my closet because it was overflowing. What am I trying to say by this? God will never leave you empty-handed and without a way of living. He won't leave you out dry in the times that we are living in because he is a faithful God. He is so faithful that I never needed to buy clothes or shoes for a few years. I kept getting clothes from different people and this went on for a couple of years.

God blesses us in abundance when we put our faith in him. His faithfulness is everlasting. We do not serve a God that is a figment of our imagination. He is the God who parted the Red Sea when Moses escaped from the Pharaoh and his army. The same God that told Moses to use his rod to part the sea is the same God who is with us every day. Job had stood firm in his faith after everything got taken away from him. God blessed him with twice as much as he had before. Back then, in the Old Testament, technology wasn't a factor like it is now. We are so advanced now that the generation of today's age lacks faith and wisdom. Our minds are so clouded and bound by the subliminal messages of the world and its practices that we turn our back on the living God. We set our eyes on fame, money and the wonders of the world and forget who died on the cross for our transgressions. He gave his life on the cross for you and I and we dismiss it. Just because we didn't witness the crucifixion doesn't mean it has any less meaning. This generation asks for proof and demands evidence. They need to see in order to believe. We cannot follow the example of the disciple, Thomas. After Jesus arose on the third day, Thomas insisted on seeing his hands to see where the holes were. In John 20:25, it says that not only did Thomas want to see his hands, but he wanted to put his finger where the nails went or else he would not believe.

Follow the example of Abraham in his obedience and trust in God through his actions of faith. Look to the perfecter and author of faith, Jesus. Put away your "I need to see to believe" mind set and walk forward believing in God's word and in his faithfulness. Although we cannot see him, he reveals himself to us if we only just look for him and keep our focus on the Lord.

Obedience

Obedience is a topic that I hardly hear preached about. Obedience is better than sacrifice. We can do all the sacrifices that we can come up with for God, but without obedience we are still actively sinning against God.

Look at the story of Jonah. Everyone knows the story of Jonah being swallowed by a big fish, not a whale. Scripture does not tell us what species of fish it was. We know all about this portion of the story, but what about what brought him to be swallowed by this big fish? The story starts off with God giving Jonah a command to go to the city of Nineveh to preach to them about their wickedness for them to repent. He fled from God on a ship. God caused a great storm to form and the people on board knew it was because of Jonah. As a result, they tossed him out to sea, where he was swallowed by the big fish. After three days and three nights, God commanded the fish to vomit him out and gave Jonah the same command for the second time to go to Nineveh. The result of his disobedience caused trouble for those around him, and he ended up being swallowed. Today, our disobedience may not cause us to be swallowed by a fish, but we cannot be living in direct disobedience of God. If God gives us a command to do something or to go somewhere, or to take action, we must obey. God has other ways to show us that disobedience is wrong. In the book of 1 Samuel 15:22, it says that to obey is better than sacrifice.

As you walk in your faithfulness to God, remember to always obey his voice when he speaks to you. He desires our faithfulness. Our obedience to him is far more important than anything else. Part of loving God is to keep his commandments. Don't turn away from his word and his commandments over our life.

The Calling

Just to recap on my life, I have a sister and a brother. It almost seems unreal to me to have so many battles occurring in my life. The enemy continues trying to withhold me from the purpose of God. I had a lot of guidance throughout the early stages of my Christian life. During this time, as a young Christian, I was living at home with my sister still there. I had seen a transformation of God's power over her life. I was always curious about her experiences, as she was always a person kept to herself. My sister has experienced many enduring trials throughout her life. She felt inspired from within herself to write something here in this book. Inspired to recount some of her experiences and what God has put in her heart to write.

My Sister Speaks:

Who is God? It depends on who you are asking. God is a title, a destination of rank. Like the word queen. What queen are you talking about? Queen Latifah? Queen Elizabeth II? Whom do you serve? It is a choice you make. You say, "I am an atheist. I believe in no god, so I serve none." Well then, you serve yourself.

I have chosen to serve the God who called to me when I was young. For a long time, I didn't know anything about him. Not even his name. I knew there was an entity outside myself that I could not see that "called" to me. There was no sound, but there was a "whisper" in my mind. I called to this entity in my darkest and most desperate times. Because there is so much confusion in this world, let me be clear, it was the spirit of the God of Abraham, Isaac, and Jacob. This Spirit had no fear in it. Only love. Peace. A warmth that reaches the depths of your being. I was desperate for its presence. I felt it in my church. Not all the time. But there were days when I felt this presence in such a powerful way. I did not want to leave. I would have lived in the church if they let me. But I didn't live there and after a day or two, things went back to normal.

My normal was not your average normal. Most nights, I was terrified. I felt things in my room. Like something was watching me. I made sure my windows were completely covered at night. I covered up every reflective surface in my room. Every mirror, every screen, every cup and fork and CDs, and anything else that reflected anything would always be covered at night. This was my personal ritual for sanity. I felt things in my room, things that I could not see. I did not want to see these things in a reflection by accident. I'm not sure if this was something someone told me to do or if I had seen a reflection of something when I was younger, but no longer remember it. Every night I did this until my family moved out of that place. It never stopped anything, but it made me feel a little bit better to do it. There was always a light on, and I kept the radio on all night. I had Christian music playing all night. I didn't want to be alone. Some nights, I had horrible experiences. There were times I experienced what felt like kicks in the stomach. There were times my hands were pulled up over my head and my legs stretched out while I was in bed and repeatedly hit by something I could not see. There were times when I could not move and felt like every muscle in my body was on fire and being shocked. There were times my mind would go completely and utterly blank. It's such a devastating feeling to not know who you are or where you are or what is happening and to only feel fear consuming you. In those times, the only thing I knew was the memory of this entity of love that I knew existed. My mind knew no words, but my spirit called out to him. My spirit cried out for him. And he would save me. Over and over again, he would save me. There were times he came gently. There were times he came like a hurricane with a fierce hand against what was in my room.

There were so many experiences. I didn't even know how to pray or who I should pray to. In his infinite mercy, he revealed himself to me. I went to church, but I didn't know anything. I went to Sunday school, so I knew the stories, but stories won't save you. They have no power. I had a Bible I did not know how to use. When I was 11, I started trying to read it. I read the words in red, thinking they are red, they must be important. I prayed the prayer of salvation. It changed nothing, so I thought I must be saying it wrong. Let me say it again... And again... many times. I really meant it with all my heart. But it changed nothing in my circumstances. However, I had made a definite decision to give my all to Him. And he was merciful to me. After a long time, I learned.

Sometimes you have to take back your freedom. God gave the promised land to his people, but it was full of giants and ungodly nations. He told them to drive them out and take what was given to them. You must take up the sword of the spirit. You must learn your weapon, and you must use it. But remember that the battle is not yours, it is God's. Victory has already been given. You already have this authority if you have surrendered to God and chosen to live in obedience to his word. You must claim it and enforce it through the exercising of your faith through verbal proclamation. Open your mouth and use your voice with authority and say what you want to be done and declare it done. While doing so, you must hold the image of it in your mind and believe that it is done. Because if the son has made you free, you will be free indeed.

But obedience is key. Do you trust God? Do you trust him with all your heart and soul? He has given us a purpose before we were ever conceived. We existed in his mind before we came to our earthly bodies. He sees our future as clearly as he sees us now. You must learn to be guided by his spirit. He has given us the Holy Spirit to teach us all things. If he tells you through his spirit to do something, don't hesitate. Even if it doesn't make sense. Trust that he sees farther than you can. Trust that his decision is for your good. There are processes in our life that can take years to complete. We are impatient. We are accustomed to getting what we want quickly. Many times, God is working on your situation in ways that you are unaware of. He is putting everything in its place to give you the blessing you've been asking for. Wait for it. Don't grow weary. Don't grow impatient. The harder it is to break through the barriers, the greater the blessing that is coming.

When you find yourself in spiritual warfare, your obedience is crucial. If the spirit moves you to anoint your home, do it. If he brings to your mind something in your home you feel as though you should get rid of, don't question it, just obey. There was a time I felt myself being woken up in the middle of the night. I look around and see no reason to be up. After several nights like this, I finally ask God to reveal the reason I am woken from my sleep. The answer immediately came to my mind. Fast. Sometimes that's all I get is one word. But Lord, how long? Fast. What should I fast for? Fast. One word and I obey. After 10 days of fasting till sundown, I hear his voice again. It is enough. After that, nothing happens for 2 weeks. Then, out of nowhere, one day I realized why it was necessary. There came a day when a situation happened where my life was in danger. On that day, I clearly heard his instructions. He would tell me when to speak, when to be silent, when to be calm, and when to move. In the end, he instructed me to do something I couldn't believe. It felt so contrary to what I thought he should be telling me, but I didn't question it. I had learned many years ago to trust him. I know for a fact I would not have been able to do as he instructed if I had not fasted those days before. I would not have the emotional strength or clarity of mind to do anything that I did that day.

When there is rebellion in your heart, you cannot be obedient. We are like the potter's clay, and he molds us to his liking. When we step out of his will and try to go our own way, he must start over. I have seen many of God's children stuck in a loop. They are unwilling to be molded. There is rebellion in their hearts. They will fight against what the spirit tries to do in their life. They want things their way. They grow angry and resentful when he does not do as they ask. They shout and say, why can't you just answer my prayer!? I fast and pray and you do nothing. You could just touch this person's heart and I would have my blessing! It's so easy, but you don't do it. All the while, God is trying to work a greater blessing for them. We see this very reaction from a man named Naaman in the book of 2 Kings Chapter 5. He was told to wash in the Jordan River 7 times to heal his skin condition, and he was angry because he wanted God's prophet to wave his hands to heal him instead. He could easily snap his fingers and all your problems would be solved, but you would learn nothing, and you would never grow. Don't allow rebellion to rule in your heart. God will bring situations into your life to humble you. It is a painful process. He will break you if he must. He loves you that much. Just like the clay, he will pound you down again to a lump and pour water over you to soften you until you are ready. He will do this as many times as it takes for you to learn. When you finally surrender, he will build you up again to be a vessel of honor.

James 4:7-10 (NKJV)

Submit yourselves therefore to God. Resist the devil and he will flee from you. Draw near to God and He will draw near to you. Cleanse your hands, you sinners; and purify your hearts, you double-minded. Lament and mourn and weep! Let your laughter be turned to mourning and your joy to gloom. Humble yourselves in the sight of the Lord, and He will lift you up.

Bible verses to reflect on in this chapter.

Hosea 6:6 (NKJV)

For I desire mercy and not sacrifice,
And the knowledge of God more than burnt offerings.

John 14:21 (NKJV)

He who has My commandments and keeps them, it is he who loves Me. And he who loves Me will be loved by My Father, and I will love him and manifest Myself to him."

2 Corinthians 3:17 (KJV)
Now the Lord is that Spirit: and where the Spirit of the Lord is, there is liberty.

John 14:26 (NKJV)
But the Helper, the Holy Spirit, whom the Father will send in My name, He will teach you all things, and bring to your remembrance all things that I said to you.

Isaiah 11:2 (NKJV)
The Spirit of the Lord shall rest upon Him, The Spirit of wisdom and understanding, The Spirit of counsel and might, The Spirit of knowledge and of the fear of the Lord.

Romans 8:26 (KJV)
Likewise the Spirit also helpeth our infirmities: for we know not what we should pray for as we ought: but the Spirit itself maketh intercession for us with groanings which cannot be uttered.

James 1:6 (NKJV)
But let him ask in faith, with no doubting, for he who doubts is like a wave of the sea driven and tossed by the wind.

Hebrews 12:2 (NKJV)
looking unto Jesus, the author and finisher of our faith, who for the joy that was set before Him endured the cross, despising the shame, and has sat down at the right hand of the throne of God.

Hebrews 11:6 (KJV)

But without faith it is impossible to please him: for he that cometh to God must believe that he is, and that he is a rewarder of them that diligently seek him.

1 Peter 1:7 (NKJV)

that the genuineness of your faith, being much more precious than gold that perishes, though it is tested by fire, may be found to praise, honor, and glory at the revelation of Jesus Christ.

James 2:17 (NKJV)

Thus also faith by itself, if it does not have works, is dead.

Psalms 107:13-14 (NKJV)

Then they cried out to the Lord in their trouble, And He saved them out of their distresses. He brought them out of darkness and the shadow of death, And broke their chains in pieces.

10

Go to the World

As you accept Jesus as your Lord and savior, God gives you authority. We are called to go into the nations of this world. Called to go across this earth to preach the word of God. We often ask ourselves to preach the word of God is to say what exactly? There are so many things to speak about, but the answer is quite simple: it's Jesus. Let us all go across nations to bring forth who Jesus was and still is. You'll be surprised by how many people in these foreign countries have never even heard about the name of Jesus. In the Bible, it calls us to preach the gospel to everyone.

Mark 16:15-18 (NKJV)

And He said to them, "Go into all the world and preach the gospel to every creature. He who believes and is baptized will be saved; but he who does not believe will be condemned. And these signs will follow those who believe: In My name they will cast out demons; they will speak with new tongues; they will take up serpents; and if they drink anything deadly, it will by no means hurt them; they will lay hands on the sick, and they will recover."

It is our mission, as followers of Christ, to reach the nations by whatever means possible. We all have a purpose to fulfill in spreading Christ throughout the world. We all work together as the body of Christ all around the world by carrying out the will of God and sharing the good news of the gospel. Some people are called to be prophets, whilst others are called with the gift of healing. In the Bible it states that there are differences in ministries and diversities of activities in the Lord. There are many functions within God's kingdom, and we are all working towards the same goal. We are all unified as one body to tell the world of Jesus Christ. This is where the different gifts of the spirit factor in each one of our different ministries. These different gifts are used to bring the word of God to the nations. I encourage you to read 1 Corinthians 12:1-11. It covers everything that I have mentioned.

The work of a missionary is going out to foreign and rugged lands to preach about Jesus. These are the people that have dedicated their lives to getting accustomed to the harsh environments. They feel from God that this is their calling. These people that do missionary work go out to places with limited transportation and resources, to rough environments to bring the gospel. This work is not for everyone, believe me, but if this is your calling, God will confirm it to you. If you are in rugged terrain, do not fear your enemy, for the Lord is with you. In the book of Acts, chapter 28, Paul had escaped a shipwreck and landed on an island. As Paul was making a fire, a venomous snake bit him in the hand. He threw the snake into the fire, knowing that it was venomous. All the native islanders expected him to perish. They waited for him to become swollen and die, but he suffered no harm from the bite. This shows the faithfulness of God in protecting Paul from danger because of his specific calling. Not everyone's calling will be the same as it was for Paul.

If you aren't called to be a missionary, it doesn't mean that you can't proclaim the word of God. In the Bible, it says to go all over the world and to preach the gospel. Nowadays, we have so much more technology than we did when our parents were born. We have the world at our fingertips. Use this to your advantage to spread Jesus throughout the world. There is no excuse for not being able to exalt Jesus on your social media. It doesn't take much to get started. Your own testimony will speak for you even if you don't have many words to say. The world will know you by your fruits. After we accept Christ into our lives, we don't stay as we are; we continue to grow in the Lord. He transforms our minds, cleanses your hearts, and teaches us to walk in his ways. He fills us with his Holy Spirit. We will quickly see the different fruits of the spirit spring forth in our lives, as it says in Galatians chapter 5. We must be a light amid the darkness on the earth. With our lives, we can testify to the power and great wonders of our Lord.

If you have the ministry of healing, some may question what this has to do with preaching the word of God. The Bible shows us examples of Christ liberating people. Throughout the gospel, we see he healed the sick, told the dead to rise, and performed miracles. By doing these things, he was setting captive people free. Sickness binds people, but Christ came to bring healing to our lives. Jesus is here to mend the brokenhearted and his healing goes beyond a superficial wound. A divine healing of your soul and spirit is something that only Jesus can do. The Bible tells us he is the truth, and the truth will set you free and if he shall make you free, you will be free indeed.

As we grow in our ministries, our attacks will also grow and intensify. The devil is out like a roaring lion looking to see who to destroy. He wishes to kill our ministries at all costs, knowing the greatness that the Lord has for each one of us. He will bring heavy attacks on some ministries more than others, depending on what you have been called by God to do on this earth. Our ministries are all different from each other. We all have different roles to play, but our purpose on this earth is the same: to spread the good word of Jesus. We must be prepared to live in the will of God because without him, we are nothing. The enemy will not wait for you to gather your thoughts. He will strike at will to see to our destruction.

We must learn to walk in the perfect will of God and not in our own will. Walking on our own will cause situations to happen that should have never happened. Heartaches and unnecessary circumstances can come from not being obedient to God's will for us. Sometimes we put ourselves in situations because we choose to walk out of his perfect will. God knows all things, but we must observe our surroundings and equip ourselves with the word of God in our minds. We must learn to trust him and his love for us. He will not give us more than we can handle, and his plans are only for our good.

> He tells us in *Jeremiah 29:11*, *"For I know the plans I have for you,"* declares the Lord, *"plans to prosper you and not to harm you, plans to give you hope and a future."*

If you are a young person reading this, maybe God has already revealed to you his plans for your life. Don't feel overwhelmed by it. If you continue to walk in his path and his perfect will, he will get you ready for your calling. Even if your calling is to just be a worshiper or singer, it will be for the glory of God. As we go through different seasons in our lives, He will mold us and prepare us for other works he has planned for us. Perhaps you may be a worship leader now, but as seasons change,

God can place you in a different position to fill a different role later in life. In the Old Testament, we see Joseph go through many positions in his life before ultimately becoming second in command to an entire nation. God has prepared a path for us to take. We must take it with our mind being set on things above, not on things on this earth. This earth is full of sin; we must not focus on earthly things but rejoice in the Lord.

You and I must be ready to speak the word of God. In the last chapter, I spoke about authority and what that pertains to in our everyday life. Now is the time to use the knowledge we have out in the field as a warrior of Christ. The word of God is life because the word is God. The Holy Spirit will lead us and guide us in our path. As warriors of Christ, we need to be ready for those people in need out in the world. It is a necessity to use discernment and to test the spirits while we are out ministering or preaching the word of God.

Take that authority and infuse it with our duty to bring Jesus across the nations. Bringing the word of God isn't just about preaching, but also about how we live our lives and how we show compassion. Jesus demonstrated his great compassion for humanity during his time on earth. No matter what our ministry is, we are all called to show compassion and to love one another. We don't need to be talking in tongues all the time to show how much of a Christian we are. It's about being like Christ. It's about loving others.

If you want to follow Christ, you can start off with being compassionate. In the book of Matthew 20:29-34, it talks about Jesus being called out by two blind men in the multitude that was following Jesus. The multitude was telling these men to quiet down, but they insisted on calling out to Jesus. It got his attention, and he asked the men what they wanted from him. It states that Jesus had compassion and touched their eyes and immediately they both received their eyesight. We seem to forget that we need to have compassion, just like Jesus did. When we see someone in need, we should not to turn them away. There are people who may never step inside a church, but they will see the love of God working through you. Let us go feed the souls and change this world with the love of Christ.

False Prophets

The world is filling itself with false prophets and false pastors. People are believing false doctrines and false leaders. As we go out to minister the love of Christ to the world, we must do this with discernment. In the Bible it says that in the last days there shall be people who love themselves, be lovers of money, and be blasphemers. People will leave their faith and give in to seducing spirits and doctrines of devils. They shall preach and go after their own lusts and turn their ears away from the truth. They will despise what is good and falsely accuse with no self-control. Wake up, warriors of Christ! Wake up and take heed of what the word of God tells us! This is what the Bible reveals to us of what the last days shall comprise.

Ephesians 5:14 NKJV
Therefore He says: "Awake, you who sleep, Arise from the dead, And Christ will give you light."

We are in the last days when people are falsely claiming to be pastors and ministers and followers of Christ. They are ravenous wolves disguised in sheep's clothing. Do not be fooled by outward appearances. On the outside, they appear to be full of knowledge and wisdom, but they are empty and rotted inside. In the book of Matthew, chapter 12:30 says that he that is not with me is against me. Those against Jesus are against God.

There is only one truth, and that is Jesus. Jesus did not preach about gaining as much money as possible. He did not preach what people know as the prosperity gospel. People will seek what sounds good to them. They will follow preachers who make them comfortable and not those who will correct them and lead them to righteousness. They will seek leaders who will tell them how to gain riches they don't have. There are pastors who are leading congregations into sin and false doctrines. There are pastors who are swaying congregations to believe that God will bless you if you give a generous offering to the church. They cater to those who desire wealth. They play with the emotions of those who are suffering financial hardships. They pretend to be righteous, but in reality, they worship money and envy the gains of others. You may have all the riches of the world, but without Jesus, you are nothing. Money cannot buy you blessings from God. Blessings are received through prayer and believing with faith, not by giving a hundred dollars.

What's worse is that the men and women of God that are supposed to be the light in the darkness, the difference in the world, are the ones that are allowing false teachings. There are churches that teach you how to speak in tongues out of the blue rather than teaching that you must be filled with the Holy Spirit. In the book of Acts, chapter two verse four shows us that after being filled with the Holy Spirit the multitude were speaking in other tongues. The Bible is clear and contradicts these ludicrous teachings that have no merit to them. Yet people remain blind and continue to follow those with no sound truth.

Some churches are teaching a New Age religion to their congregation. There are pastors who are allowing certain practices into their churches that God condemns. All it takes is the smallest introduction of these practices to taint the whole church. As it says in Galatians 5:9, a little leaven leavens the whole lump. We, as warriors of Christ, must break the bondage of those who sleep. The deceit has deeply rooted in them, and we must open their eyes to it.

In order to go out and minister the word of God, we must understand the times that we are living in right now. We need to have awareness of what you and I are up against.

The deceit and evil practices infiltrating the church need to be rebuked and cast out in Jesus' name. We are called to spread the gospel of Christ throughout nations worldwide. Called to testify of the power and authority that God has. Yes, they will hate you, for they hated Jesus first before they hated you and me. The world loves their own and because we are not from this world, the world will hate us. The price to pay for the cause of spreading Jesus is hatred and persecution.

Jesus shed his blood on the cross for our sins. Take the shield of faith and the sword of the spirit and prepare yourself for the ministry that God has for you. Be the light in the midst of the darkness. Speak the truth and speak life to those who need to be revived. Let the Holy Spirit guide you and use you to minister to the world. The Holy Spirit is here to comfort us, teach us and guide us.

Bible verses to reflect in this chapter:

John 15:18-19 (NKJV)

If the world hates you, you know that it hated Me before it hated you. If you were of the world, the world would love its own. Yet because you are not of the world, but I chose you out of the world, therefore the world hates you.

2 Timothy 3:1-5 (KJV)

This know also, that in the last days perilous times shall come.For men shall be lovers of their own selves, covetous, boasters, proud, blasphemers, disobedient to parents, unthankful, unholy, Without natural affection, trucebreakers, false accusers, incontinent, fierce, despisers of those that are good, Traitors, heady, highminded, lovers of pleasures more than lovers of God; Having a form of godliness, but denying the power thereof: from such turn away.

2 Timothy 4:1-4 (KJV)

I charge thee therefore before God, and the Lord Jesus Christ, who shall judge the quick and the dead at his appearing and his kingdom; Preach the word; be instant in season, out of season; reprove, rebuke, exhort with all longsuffering and doctrine. For the time will come when they will not endure sound doctrine; but after their own lusts shall they heap to themselves teachers, having itching ears; And they shall turn away their ears from the truth, and shall be turned unto fables.

1 Timothy 4:1(KJV)

Now the Spirit speaketh expressly, that in the latter times some shall depart from the faith, giving heed to seducing spirits, and doctrines of devils;

Matthew 7:15 (KJV)

Beware of false prophets, which come to you in sheep's clothing, but inwardly they are ravening wolves.

Psalms 146:7-10 (NKJV)

Who executes justice for the oppressed, Who gives food to the hungry. The Lord gives freedom to the prisoners. The Lord opens the eyes of the blind; The Lord raises those who are bowed down; The Lord loves the righteous. The Lord watches over the strangers; He relieves the fatherless and widow; But the way of the wicked He turns upside down. The Lord shall reign forever— Your God, O Zion, to all generations. Praise the Lord!

Colossians 3:2 (KJV)

Set your mind on things above, not on things on earth

Romans 12:4-8 (NKJV)

For as we have many members in one body, but all the members do not have the same function, so we, being many, are one body in Christ, and individually members of one another. Having then gifts differing according to the grace that is given to us, let us use them: if prophecy, let us prophesy in proportion to our faith; or ministry, let us use it in our ministering; he who teaches, in teaching; he who exhorts, in exhortation; he who gives, with liberality; he who leads, with diligence; he who shows mercy, with cheerfulness.

1 Corinthians 12: 8-10

for to one is given the word of wisdom through the Spirit, to another the word of knowledge through the same Spirit, to another faith by the same Spirit, to another gifts of healings by the same Spirit, to another the working of miracles, to another prophecy, to another discerning of spirits, to another different kinds of tongues, to another the interpretation of tongues.

98

11

Come to Jesus

Those who read this book till the end have uncovered many deceptions of this world. Some deception has made its way into our lives and some has even made its way into our churches. Warriors of Christ, we must come together. We must unite to conquer and defeat evil with the mighty sword of the spirit. We must go to those who need the word of God. Advance to fulfill your purpose on this earth. Move towards the will of God to reach the nations. Let your testimony and fruits of the Holy Spirit bring conviction to those that lay sleeping. May the word of God cast off the false teachings of the world and bring forth a nation with a passion for Christ. Let our praise and faith gratify our Lord and Savior. We are the body of Christ. We need to preach the truth and not teach on our own accord. Put away your disbelief and pursue the righteous path of God and follow in the steps that Jesus took. Set aside all idolatry and false gods and seek the true living God.

I have referenced a vast amount of scripture throughout this book. Day after day passes and the flowers may wither, but the word of God will remain. The word of God will never change since the word is God and

God will always remain the same yesterday, today, and forevermore. Humanity changes and we fail over and over. There is one who has died for us and who has never failed, and his name is Jesus. He was the Messiah and came to bring us salvation through his sacrifice. Many people don't even believe he was the Messiah, the son of God sent for you and for me. This is real, and we must wake up, dig deep and evaluate our relationship with God.

With our lives advancing day to day, we see the popularity of new music secular artists rising. We see the world giving birth to satanic rituals done live on T. V. and see them ridiculing Jesus and even ridiculing his crucifixion. We all need to open our eyes to what is really being shown for the world to see.

Let me ask you a question: why is Jesus mocked if he was never real? Why would the world shame those who believe in Christ but on the other side be the same people glorifying the devil in videos for young children to see? I'll tell you why. We are not of this world; the world will hate us for choosing Jesus, as it says in the book of John 15:18-20. The world hated Jesus before they hated you and me for believing in him. They will mock us, shame us, and persecute us for his name's sake.

Open your eyes and ears to what is happening all around us. There needs to be an awakening throughout this nation! You must choose to serve Jesus or to serve the world. You will love one and hate the other. Who will you choose? We cannot serve two masters. If you deny Jesus, he will deny you. You have free will to do as you please, but remember this; life is not guaranteed, and we do not know when our time will be up in this world. You may be fine now, but tomorrow you may die without even seeing it coming. Will you be ready to reap the consequence of the life that you have chosen for yourself by denying Jesus? Do not let so much time go without trying to look for God. Do not ignore him and say, oh I'll look for God another day. Another day is never guaranteed in life. Do not delay, the calling of God is upon your life. Perhaps you already are a devoted Christian. The question is, have you accepted Christ in your life?

In the Bible, it says that we have been bought at a price. The wages of sin is death, but the sins of humanity have been forgiven through Christ's sacrifice. Jesus came for all of us to come to repentance. He did not come only for the righteous, but for sinners as well. Salvation is there for all who want it. Jesus has already done the rest for us. You just have to be willing to submit and give your heart to God. Surrender your all to Christ and you will see a life that you have never experienced before. If you already have Christ, then I encourage you to spread the love of Jesus so that others may follow. Be bold and talk to one person about the gospel. Let God use you for his glory. If you allow God to work in your life, he will take you to places you never imagined. Declare life into people, proclaim the good works of the Lord.

I pray and hope that God has touched you and opened the eyes of many through this book. I declare a transformation in everyone's lives that this book may reach. Declaring an awakening throughout this nation and that God may bless everyone reading this. I pray our nation becomes hungry for the presence of God and that they may seek his truth. Amen.

Bible verses to reflect on.

Luke 5:32 (KJV)
I came not to call the righteous, but sinners to repentance.

1 Corinthians 6:20 (KJV)

For ye are bought with a price: therefore glorify God in your body, and in your spirit, which are God's.

Matthew 10:22 (KJV)

And ye shall be hated of all men for my name's sake: but he that endureth to the end shall be saved.

Matthew 10:33(KJV)

But whosoever shall deny me before men, him will I also deny before my Father which is in heaven.

Matthew 6:24 (KJV)

No man can serve two masters: for either he will hate the one, and love the other; or else he will hold to the one, and despise the other. Ye cannot serve God and mammon.

Resources

If you ever need someone to talk to or in need of aid for your mental health, I encourage you to visit these websites listed below.

For any crisis or mental health, the national suicide and crisis holiness number is 988 for 24 hours a day and seven days a week in the US. You may also text TALK to 741741

American foundation for suicide prevention.
  https://afsp.org/

https://floridasuicideprevention.org/

National alliance of mental illness
  https://www.nami.org/home

Online therapists range from $60-90 per week for this website.
  https://www.betterhelp.com

Another online therapists.
  https://www.talkspace.com/

Bible Verses to Study

All verses are in (KJV).

TIMES OF TROUBLE / STRONG TOWER

PSALMS 118:5

I called upon the Lord in distress: the Lord answered me, and set me in a large place.

PSALMS 18:19

He brought me forth also into a large place; he delivered me, because he delighted in me.

PSALMS 4:1

Hear me when I call, O God of my righteousness: you have enlarged me when I was in distress; have mercy upon me, and hear my prayer.

PSALMS 27:5

For in the time of trouble He shall hide me in His pavilion; In the secret place of His tabernacle He shall hide me; He shall set me high upon a rock.

PSALMS 91:1

He who dwells in the secret place of the most High shall abide under the shadow of the Almighty.

PSALMS 40:2

He brought me up also out of an horrible pit, out of the miry clay, and set my feet upon a rock, and established my steps.

PSALMS 107:6

Then they cried unto the Lord in their trouble, and he delivered them out of their distresses.

PROVERBS 18:10

The name of the Lord is a strong tower; the righteous run into it, and is safe.

PSALMS 9:9

The Lord also will be a refuge for the oppressed, a refuge in the times of trouble.

PSALMS 46:1

GOD is our refuge and strength, a very present help in trouble.

PSALMS 23:4

Yea, though I walk through the valley of the shadow of death, I will fear no evil: for thou art with me; thy rod and thy staff they comfort me.

PSALMS 54:1-2

Save me, O God, by thy name, and judge me by thy strength. Hear my prayer, O God; give ear to the words of my mouth.

2 SAMUEL 22:2-3

And he said, The Lord is my rock, and my fortress, and my deliverer; The God of my rock; in him will I trust: he is my shield, and the horn of my salvation, my high tower, and my refuge, my saviour; thou savest me from violence.

SPIRITUAL WARFARE

2 CORINTHIANS 10:3-5

For though we walk in the flesh, we do not war according to the flesh.For the weapons of our warfare are not carnal but mighty in God for pulling down strongholds,casting down arguments and every high thing that exalts itself against the knowledge of God, bringing every thought into captivity to the obedience of Christ.

LUKE 10:19

Behold, I give unto you power to tread on serpents and scorpions, and over all the power of the enemy: and nothing shall by any means hurt you.

ROMANS 6:23

For the wages of sin is death; but the gift of God is eternal life through Jesus Christ our Lord.

PHILIPPIANS 2:9-11

Wherefore God also hath highly exalted him, and given him a name which is above every name:

That at the name of Jesus every knee should bow, of things in heaven, and things in earth, and things under the earth; And that every tongue should confess that Jesus Christ is Lord, to the glory of God the Father.

EPHESIANS 6:12-18

For we wrestle not against flesh and blood, but against principalities, against powers, against the rulers of the darkness of this world, against spiritual wickedness in high places. Wherefore take unto you the whole armour of God, that ye may be able to withstand in the evil day, and having done all, to stand. Stand therefore, having your loins girt about with truth, and having on the breastplate of righteousness; And your feet shod with the preparation of the gospel of peace; Above all, taking the shield of faith, wherewith ye shall be able to quench all the fiery darts of the wicked. And take the helmet of salvation, and the sword of the Spirit, which is the word of God:Praying always with all prayer and supplication in the Spirit, and watching thereunto with all perseverance and supplication for all saints;

1 THESSALONIANS 5:8

But let us, who are of the day, be sober, putting on the breastplate of faith and love; and for an helmet, the hope of salvation.

HEBREWS 4:12

For the word of God is quick, and powerful, and sharper than any twoedged sword, piercing even to the dividing asunder of soul and spirit, and of the joints and marrow, and is a discerner of the thoughts and intents of the heart.

ISAIAH 49:2

And he hath made my mouth like a sharp sword; in the shadow of his hand hath he hid me, and made me a polished shaft; in his quiver hath he hid me;

1 TIMOTHY 6:12

Fight the good fight of faith, lay hold on eternal life, whereunto thou art also called, and hast professed a good profession before many witnesses.

STRENGTH

ISAIAH 41:10

Fear thou not; for I am with thee: be not dismayed; for I am thy God: I will strengthen thee; yea, I will help thee; yea, I will uphold thee with the right hand of my righteousness.

ISAIAH 40:31

But they that wait upon the Lord shall renew their strength; they shall mount up with wings as eagles; they shall run, and not be weary; and they shall walk, and not faint.

PHILIPPIANS 4:13

I can do all things through Christ which strengtheneth me.

DEUTERONOMY 31:6

Be strong and of a good courage, fear not, nor be afraid of them: for the Lord thy God, he it is that doth go with thee; he will not fail thee, nor forsake thee.

EXODUS 15:2

The Lord is my strength and song, and he is become my salvation: he is my God, and I will prepare him an habitation; my father's God, and I will exalt him.

JOSHUA 1:9

Have not I commanded thee? Be strong and of a good courage; be not afraid, neither be thou dismayed: for the Lord thy God is with thee whithersoever thou goest.

HABAKKUK 3:19

The Lord God is my strength, and he will make my feet like hinds' feet, and he will make me to walk upon mine high places. To the chief singer on my stringed instruments.

EPHESIANS 6:10

Finally, my brethren, be strong in the Lord, and in the power of his might.

ISAIAH 40:29

He giveth power to the faint; and to them that have no might he increaseth strength.

2 CORINTHIANS 12:10

Therefore I take pleasure in infirmities, in reproaches, in necessities, in persecutions, in distresses for Christ's sake: for when I am weak, then am I strong.

Notes

DATE   /   /

DATE   /   /

DATE / /

DATE / /